VEGAN RECIPES FROM FRANCE

KRISTINA ARNOLD

GRUB STREET | LONDON

CONTENTS

French Cuisine page 6

Recipes page 11

BASICS
page 13

STARTERS
page 33

MAIN COURSES
page 57

DESSERTS
page 117

Index page 166

FRENCH CUISINE

Cuisine Française

Since the fifteenth century, the cuisine of France has been the most influential in Europe. It was at that time that the first cookery books were printed in the French language.

In the seventeenth and eighteenth centuries, the French court was considered to be the most culturally advanced, and as a result, the French style of cooking was adopted by the kitchens of many noble houses throughout Europe. It was the origin of the traditional sequence of soup main course and dessert typical of Western meals, and of set meals consisting of multiple courses.

Food has always been an important part in the daily life of the French, even today. At the time of the French Revolution, an increasing number of restaurants were opened, giving the middle classes greater access to the finest culinary arts. Cooks established standards of preparation and quality for the dishes they served in their restaurants. This newly developed 'grande cuisine' spread around the country and abroad, becoming renowned the world over. Great importance was attached to culinary pleasure, particularly among the upper classes.

Haute cuisine originated in the nineteenth century and developed into the French national cuisine. It is characterised by its very high quality and versatility. However, many different styles of regional cooking can also be found throughout the country, making use of local produce, combinations of ingredients and preparatory methods. Among the best-known styles of regional cooking are those of Normandy, Brittany and Provence. In simple terms, the food in the south of France is Mediterranean in style, while that of the inland regions is heartier.

French cuisine is often associated with *l'art de vivre*, the art of living. This book intends to show how this art can also be fully enjoyed in its vegan version. With this in mind, we wish you *bonne chance* and *bon appétit*!

RECIPES

All recipes serve four people.
The appropriate information is given where there are any exceptions.

BASICS

Baguette   page 14
Brioches   page 16
Apricot croissants   page 18
Aïoli   page 20
Vegetable stock   page 22
Olive paste   page 24
Provençal pesto   page 26
Vinaigrette   page 26
Fromage frais   page 28
Béchamel sauce   page 30

BAGUETTE

TIME REQUIRED: *1 hour + 6 hours resting time*

Makes 6

*1 kg plain flour
2 sachets dry yeast
750 ml lukewarm water
3–4 tsp salt*

'Baguette' is the French word for a stick, most likely a reference to its long and slender shape.

1. Combine the dry ingredients well, add the water and mix thoroughly. Use a hand mixer [fitted with a dough hook] to knead the dough until it is smooth and comes away from the side of the bowl. Dust the dough with a little flour, cover with a cloth and rest in a warm place for about 6 hours.

2. On a floured pastry board, knead the dough well and divide into 6 pieces. Knead each piece again and roll up into a sausage.

3. Line baking trays with baking parchment and lay 3 baguettes on each tray with the join tucked underneath. Cover again and rest for 10 minutes. Preheat the oven to 240°C/475°F/gas 9.

4. Slash each baguette several times along its length on the diagonal with a sharp knife and brush with water. With the oven shelf on the second position from the bottom, bake for 15 minutes. Then lower the temperature to 200°C/400°F/gas 6 and bake for 30 more minutes.

Tip: Baguettes are traditionally only made using wheat flour, yeast, water and salt. For a little variety, the only additional ingredients allowed are less than two per cent broad bean flour, soya flour or malted wheat flour.

BRIOCHES

TIME REQUIRED: *1 hour*

Makes 30 brioches

500 g plain flour
30 g fresh yeast
6 tablespoons lukewarm soya milk
2 tsp sugar
150 g high-quality vegan margarine
4 tbsp soya yoghurt
½ tsp salt
Vegan cream, for glazing
Vegan margarine, for greasing

Brioches are believed to have originated in Normandy. What makes these brioches special is that a small ball of yeast dough is set on top of a larger one like a pyramid.

1. Grease the brioche moulds well with margarine at room temperature.
2. To make the sponge starter, sift some flour into a bowl, make a well and crumble the yeast into it. Mix with soya milk, sugar and a little more flour. Cover with a cotton cloth and rest in a warm place for about 15 minutes.
3. Melt the margarine and leave it to cool. Mix it with the flour, soya yoghurt and salt. Mix all the ingredients together. Knead the dough with your hands until it becomes elastic. Cover again and leave to rise for 15 minutes.
4. Knead the dough well, divide in half and roll each half into a sausage. Cut both sausages into 15 pieces of uniform size. Roll each piece into a large and a small ball. Put each of the large balls into the moulds and press down with your thumb to make an indentation. Brush inside with a little vegan cream (you can also add a little jam if you like). Gently press a small ball into the indentation. Glaze the brioches with the vegan cream. Rest them for 10 more minutes.
5. Preheat the oven to 220°C/425°F/gas 7. Put the moulds on a baking tray and, with the oven shelf on the second position from the bottom, bake for 15–20 minutes, until golden. Transfer to a rack and leave to cool.

Tip: If you don't have brioche moulds, you can shape the brioches and place them directly on the baking sheet. They may not look as nice when they're done, but they'll taste just as good!

APRICOT CROISSANTS

Croissants à l'Abricot

TIME REQUIRED:
25 minutes
+ about 12 hours cooling and resting time

Makes 8

500 g vegan leavened laminated (croissant or Danish pastry) dough
8 tbsp apricot jam
Vegan cream, for glazing

For the dough:
225 g flour
1 pinch salt
20 g sugar
½ sachet dry yeast
75 ml soya milk
80 ml cold water
10 g high-quality vegan margarine, melted

125 g high-quality vegan margarine, cold
1 tsp plain flour

Croissants are said to be named after the crescent moon, which they resemble. Although they're time-consuming to make, you'll be rewarded by their incomparably soft and flaky texture.

1. Combine the milk and water in a bowl. Mix the flour, salt, sugar and yeast separately and add to the mixture. Finally, add the melted margarine. Knead briefly with a mixer fitted with a dough hook on low speed for about 1 minute (add a little water or flour if necessary). Roll the dough into a ball, transfer to a bowl greased with oil and rest for at least 6 hours in the refrigerator.

2. Next, cut the cold margarine into small pieces and knead with a teaspoon of flour. Work quickly to prevent the margarine becoming too soft. Put the margarine on a sheet of aluminium foil and shape into a 15-cm square about 5 mm in thickness. Wrap it in foil and rest in the refrigerator for 1 hour.

3. Roll out the dough on a floured work surface into roughly 30 x 20-cm rectangle. Lay the margarine square on the left side of the dough and fold the right side over to encase it. Seal the edges well. Use a rolling pin to carefully roll out the dough into a 40 x 20-cm sheet. Fold the right and left edges over into the middle and rest in the refrigerator for about 30 minutes.

4. Place the dough on a floured work surface. Carefully roll it out again to a 40 x 20-cm sheet then fold it into thirds. Rest in the refrigerator for 30 minutes and then repeat the operation. Then refrigerate the dough for 20 more minutes.

Basics

5. Roll out the dough into a 30-cm-diameter circle. Cut the circle into 8 wedges (like pizza slices). Put 1 teaspoon of apricot jam in the centre of a wedge and roll it up from the bottom, turning the pointed sides slightly inwards. Tuck the end under the croissant, pressing firmly, to prevent it from coming loose while baking. Rest the croissants 2-3 hours on a baking tray lined with baking parchment.

6. Preheat the oven to 180°C/350°F/gas 4. Brush the croissants with a little vegan cream to give them a nice golden colour when baked. Bake for 20–25 minutes on the middle shelf, until golden.

AÏOLI

TIME REQUIRED:
10 minutes

80 g white sandwich bread, crust removed and soaked in a little water
200 ml extra-virgin olive oil
6 cloves garlic
Salt, pepper

Aïoli hails from Marseille. A grand aïoli is a feast and social occasion to be shared by family and friends.

1. Squeeze the bread, break it into small pieces and put it into a blending beaker. Peel and coarsely chop the garlic and add it to the bread.
2. Use a hand-held blender to incorporate the oil, first a drop at a time and then in a stream. If the aïoli is too thick, thin it with a little soya yoghurt.

VEGETABLE STOCK

Bouillon de Légumes

TIME REQUIRED: *2 hours*

*1 kg assorted vegetables
(onions, carrots, celery,
fennel, etc.)*
2 litres water

Stock is an essential ingredient, particularly for vegan cooking.

1. According to availability and preference, wash, clean and coarsely chop the vegetables.
2. Combine with the water in a large pan. Bring to the boil, lower the heat, cover and simmer for about 2 hours.

OLIVE PASTE

Pâte d'Olive

TIME REQUIRED:
10 minutes

70 g pitted black olives
20 g capers
1 tsp Dijon mustard
3 tbsp olive oil
Salt, pepper

1. Coarsely chop the olives and capers and combine in a blending beaker with the mustard. Purée with a hand-held blender while gradually incorporating the oil.
2. Season with salt and pepper.

Tip: Olives are green before they ripen, later darkening and turning black. The tastiest are the small, black Niçoise olives.

PROVENÇAL PESTO

TIME REQUIRED:
10 minutes

100 ml extra-virgin olive oil
40 g pine nuts
1 bunch basil
5 cloves garlic
1 tsp yeast flakes
Salt, pepper

THE ORIGINAL RECIPE for pesto, *pistou* in French, consists of only olive oil, fresh basil and garlic.

1. Crush the solid ingredients into a thick paste in a mortar.
2. Mix in the oil in a thin stream to make a thick sauce.
3. Season with salt.

VINAIGRETTE

2 tbsp red wine vinegar
7 tbsp olive oil
1 tsp Dijon mustard
1 pinch sugar
1 tsp salt
Pepper

THE WORD *VINAIGRE*, the French word for vinegar, literally means 'sour wine'. The better the quality of the wine, the better the quality of the vinegar.

1. Mix the vinegar with the mustard, sugar, salt and pepper.
2. Add the oil in a thin stream while whisking with a hand mixer to give the dressing a creamy consistency.

FROMAGE FRAIS

TIME REQUIRED:
30 minutes

1 litre soya milk
3 tsp apple cider vinegar
3 tsp lemon juice
Salt, pepper
Vegan cream (optional)

BECAUSE THIS FRESH cheese has a very neutral flavour, it can be used as a filling for different tarts.

1. Combine the soya milk with the apple cider vinegar and lemon juice in a pan and bring to the boil. Lower the heat and simmer for about 10 minutes, stirring constantly, until the mixture curdles.
2. Pour it into a large sieve lined with a cloth, and then twist the ends of the cloth together. Keep squeezing the contents well until you're left with a solid mass inside the cloth. Transfer the cheese to a bowl and season with salt and pepper. Mix in a little vegan cream, if desired.

BÉCHAMEL SAUCE

TIME REQUIRED:
15 minutes

100 g high-quality vegan margarine
4 level tbsp plain flour
1 litre soya milk
Salt, pepper

ONE OF THE traditional basic sauces, béchamel is highly valued in French cuisine.

1. Melt the margarine in a pan and whisk in the flour without browning.

2. Gradually stir in the soya milk. Leave to simmer gently, but don't forget to stir! Otherwise, the béchamel will quickly stick to the bottom of the pan. The consistency (the sauce should be thick rather than thin) depends on the amount of liquid you add. You must also stir the sauce constantly when reheating it.

STARTERS

French onion soup   page 34
Tomato soup with rosemary foam   page 36
Chestnut soup   page 38
Artichoke purée with baguette and olive paste   page 40
Artichokes with two dips   page 42
Herbes de Provence and almond terrine with beetroot salad   page 44
Vegetable terrine with marinated spring onions   page 46
Pear and fennel salad with caramelised nuts and grapes   page 48
Leek soup   page 50
Bitter salad with apple and juniper vinaigrette   page 52
Tomato sorbet with basil   page 54

FRENCH ONION SOUP

Soupe à l'Oignon Française

TIME REQUIRED: *2 hours*

For the soup:
750 g onions
3 tbsp sunflower oil
2 tbsp olive oil
1 pinch sugar
½ tsp salt
1 level tbsp flour
1½ litres vegetable broth
200 ml white wine
Salt, pepper

For the garnish:
8 (about 1-cm thick) slices baguette (see recipe on page 14)
2 cloves garlic
2 tbsp olive oil
125 g grated vegan cheese

A Parisian speciality. In the old days, early risers and people going home after a night out would head for the old produce market of Les Halles, known as 'the belly of Paris', to fortify themselves with this soup.

1. Peel and slice the onions very thinly.

2. Heat both oils together in a pan over a medium heat. Add the onions and sauté for 5 minutes, until translucent. Cover and cook over a low heat for about 15 minutes, stirring often. Add the sugar and salt and sauté, uncovered, for 20 more minutes, until the onions turn golden brown.

3. Stir in the flour and brown for 3–4 minutes. Slowly pour in the hot broth and bring the soup to a boil, stirring well from time to time. Add the wine and season with freshly ground pepper. Turn down the heat, cover and simmer for 30–40 more minutes, until the onions start to fall apart.

4. Toast the baguette slices. Rub the surface with the halved garlic cloves and olive oil.

5. Preheat the oven to 240°C/475°F/gas 9 (or simply use the grill). Divide the soup into 4 ovenproof dishes. Cover with 2 slices of toast and sprinkle with grated cheese. Place the bowls on a baking tray lined with baking parchment and place in the top third of the oven until the cheese turns golden brown. Serve immediately.

Tip: The thinner the onions, the better.

TOMATO SOUP WITH ROSEMARY FOAM

Soupe de Tomate à la Mousse de Romarin

TIME REQUIRED:
30 minutes

For the soup:
600 g very ripe tomatoes
450 g tinned peeled tomatoes + liquid
1 tbsp olive oil
2 shallots
5 cloves garlic
2 bay leaves
1 tsp dried oregano
2 sprigs thyme
200 ml water
Salt, pepper

For the rosemary foam:
200 ml soya milk
1 sprig rosemary
1 pinch salt
Pepper

Rosemary means 'dew of the sea'. Rosemary grows particularly well in the salty air of the Mediterranean region.

1. Score the tomatoes with a cross, put them into a pan and pour boiling water over them. Take them out after about 5 minutes, peel and coarsely dice.
2. Peel and finely dice the shallots and garlic. Heat the oil in a pan and sauté the shallots and garlic. Add the tomatoes, sauté briefly and turn down the heat. Simmer for 15 minutes and then add the tinned tomatoes with their liquid and the herbs. Stir well and add the water. Simmer for 10 more minutes.
3. Purée the soup with a hand-held blender and season with salt and pepper. Warm serving bowls and have them ready.
4. For the rosemary foam, add the rosemary to the soya milk in a pan and heat until close to the boil. Then whisk until frothy. Serve the soup with the rosemary foam.

Starters

CHESTNUT SOUP

Soupe de Châtaignes

TIME REQUIRED:
60 minutes

200 g chestnuts, roasted, peeled and chopped
150 g potatoes
1 onion
100 g celeriac
100 g carrots
50 g fennel
1 tbsp muscovado sugar
1 tbsp apple cider vinegar
4 peppercorns
5 juniper berries
2 bay leaves
1 pinch ground cloves
1 litre water

Chestnuts were once considered the 'bread of the poor'. Particularly in the early Middle Ages, they were a dietary staple.

1. Wash, peel and coarsely dice the potatoes. Clean and dice the celeriac, carrots and fennel. Peel and finely dice the onion.

2. Melt the sugar in a large pan. Deglaze the pan with the vinegar and add water. Stir well with a whisk. Add the vegetables, spices and the chopped chestnuts and bring to the boil. Then turn down the heat. Simmer for about 45 minutes, stirring often until all the vegetables are very soft. Add more water if necessary.

3. Purée the soup with a hand blender or strain through a sieve and season with salt.

Starters

ARTICHOKE PURÉE WITH BAGUETTE AND OLIVE PASTE

PURÉE AUX ARTICHAUTS SUR BAGUETTE AVEC PÂTE D'OLIVE

TIME REQUIRED:
10 minutes

180 g artichoke hearts in oil, drained
250 g tinned chickpeas, drained
150 g basil leaves
1 tsp salt
Pepper

1 baguette (see recipe on page 14)
1 serving olive paste (see recipe on page 24)

ARTICHOKES ARE PRACTICALLY the emblem of Brittany and Normandy. They were introduced into France by Catherine de' Medici in the sixteenth century.

1. Combine the artichoke hearts, chickpeas, basil, salt and pepper in a blending beaker and purée with a hand blender. Refrigerate until ready to serve.
2. Serve with a freshly baked baguette and the olive paste.

ARTICHOKES WITH TWO DIPS
Artichauts avec Deux Trempettes

TIME REQUIRED:
50 minutes

2 large or 4 small artichokes
1 tbsp lemon juice
1 tbsp salt
About 2 litres water

1 serving aïoli (see recipe on page 20)
1 serving olive paste (see recipe on page 24)

The artichokes grown in Brittany and Normandy are large and fleshy fruits with green, rounded and notched leaves.

1. Rinse the artichokes in cold water. Twist and break off the stalks. This will pull away the tough fibres that keep the leaves upright.
2. Bring the water to the boil in a large pan and add the lemon juice and salt. Put the artichokes into the pan (you may need 2 pans) stalk-side down. Cook over a medium heat for 30–50 minutes (depending on size). The artichokes are ready to eat when a leaf can be easily pulled out.
3. Take them out and leave to cool a little.
4. In the meantime, make the aïoli and olive paste. Serve them with the artichokes. To eat the artichoke, carefully pull out the leaves, dip and pull the bottom third of the leaf between your teeth. Remove the choke (fine hairs) from the centre of the artichokes and eat the heart with aïoli.

HERBES DE PROVENCE AND ALMOND TERRINE WITH BEETROOT SALAD

Terrine aux Herbes de Provence, Amandes et Salade de Betteraves Rouges

TIME REQUIRED:
40 minutes + 6 hours refrigeration time

Small loaf tin (15 x 8 cm)

For the terrine:
400 g soya yoghurt (250 g drained)
1 tbsp maple syrup
30 g slivered almonds
60 g chestnuts, roasted and peeled
120 g grapes, if possible small and seedless
2½ tsp Herbes de Provence
1 sachet agar-agar
150 g soya cream
1 tbsp whipped cream stabiliser
1 tbsp lemon juice
Salt, pepper

Herbes de Provence is the name given to a blend of dried herbs containing basil, thyme, fennel, savory and lavender flowers that is ready to use.

1. Leave the yoghurt to drain overnight in a cloth-lined sieve.

2. Heat the maple syrup in a pan, add the slivered almonds and stir until caramelised. Transfer to a sheet of baking parchment and separate the slivers with a fork. Leave to cool.

3. Cut the chestnuts into 2-mm-thick slices. Wash and pluck the grapes. Finely chop the rosemary and sage, and pluck the thyme leaves [if using in place of the Herbes de Provence, see **Tip** opposite].

4. In a pan, dissolve the agar-agar in 50 ml of water and simmer for 2 minutes. Stir in 2 tablespoons of the yoghurt and then mix in with well with the remaining yoghurt. Stir in the herbs and loosely fold in the grapes, chestnuts and almonds.

5. Finally, whip the cream with the stabiliser and carefully stir into the mixture. Season with salt, pepper and lemon juice.

6. Pour the mixture into a small loaf tin (15 x 8 cm) lined with cling film. Cover with cling film and refrigerate for at least 6 hours.

7. Wash the beetroot, cover with water in a pan and bring to the boil. Turn down the heat and simmer for 40–50 minutes. Prick the beetroot with a fork. If it's soft, drain and refresh in cold water. Peel, slice and season with nutmeg, caraway seeds, salt, pepper, sugar, vinegar and oil.

For the salad:
400 g beetroot
1 pinch ground nutmeg
1 tsp caraway seeds
1 pinch sugar
4 tbsp red wine vinegar
6 tbsp olive oil
Salt, pepper

8. Carefully turn out and slice the terrine and serve with the beetroot salad.

Tip: Instead of Herbes de Provence, you can also use 4 small sprigs of thyme (or 1 tsp dried), 1 tbsp rosemary leaves (or 1 tsp dried) and 3 sage leaves (or ½ tsp dried).

VEGETABLE TERRINE WITH MARINATED SPRING ONIONS

Terrine de Légumes et Oignons de Printemps Marinés

TIME REQUIRED:
30 minutes + 8 hours refrigeration time

Terrine mould (15 x 8 cm)

For the terrine:
200 ml vegetable stock (see recipe on page 22)
3 cloves garlic
100 g broccoli
130 g cauliflower
50 g courgettes
3 small carrots
1 spring onion
1 tbsp olive oil
Salt, pepper
1 sachet agar-agar

For the marinated onions:
4 spring onions
Juice of ½ lemon
2 tbsp olive oil
Salt, pepper

Terrine was originally the name given to an earthenware mould used to make pies. However, terrines are also dishes that are cooked without pastry or, as here, chilled.

1. Make the vegetable stock.

2. Peel and chop the garlic. Wash, trim and chop up the remaining vegetables. Heat the olive oil in a frying pan and sauté the vegetables until translucent. Add 100 ml of water and cook for 10 minutes. Season with salt and pepper. Mix the stock with the gelling agent and bring to the boil for 2 minutes while stirring constantly. Remove from the heat, leave to cool a little and stir in the cooked vegetables.

3. Transfer the vegetables and stock to a terrine mould (15 x 8 cm) lined with cling film. Cover with cling film and refrigerate for at least 8 hours.

4. Slice the spring onions and marinate in a mixture of the lemon juice, olive oil, salt and pepper. Slice the terrine and serve with marinated spring onions.

STARTERS
46

PEAR AND FENNEL SALAD WITH CARAMELISED NUTS AND GRAPES

Salade de Poire et Fenouil aux Noix et Raisins Caramélisés

TIME REQUIRED:
20 minutes

1 pear
1 fennel bulb
1 orange
150 ml freshly squeezed orange juice
2–3 tbsp oil
8 caper berries
100 g muscovado sugar
24 grapes
16 walnut halves
Salt
Pepper
4 sprigs thyme or peppermint

Walnuts are valued for their flavour and nutritional value. More than 40 per cent of their fat content consists of polyunsaturated fatty acids.

1. Wash the pear and fennel and slice lengthways, removing the core.
2. Peel and slice the orange.
3. Mix the orange juice with the oil and season with salt and pepper.
4. Combine the pear, fennel and orange in a bowl with the caper berries and pour over the orange juice marinade. Leave to stand.
5. Make a light caramel with the sugar in a frying pan (don't allow the caramel to darken as it will taste bitter).
6. Toss the grapes and walnuts in the caramel and leave to cool on a sheet of baking parchment.
7. Serve the salad on plates and garnish with the grapes and nuts. Decorate with thyme or peppermint.

LEEK SOUP

Soupe aux Poireaux

TIME REQUIRED:
45 minutes

300 g leeks
1 medium onion
2 cloves garlic
1 tbsp plain flour
1 tbsp high-quality vegan margarine
1 litre water
Salt, pepper
Vegan cream (optional)

A DISTINCTION IS made between summer leeks, which are light green, tender and mild, and winter leeks, available from September, which are dark green and somewhat coarser.

1. Wash, trim and slice the leeks into 2-mm-thick rings. Peel and slice the onion into rings. Peel and finely chop the garlic.

2. Melt the margarine in a large pan and stir in the flour until light brown. Deglaze the pan with the water and stir well with a whisk. Add the leeks, onion and garlic, and bring to the boil. Then turn down the heat and simmer, covered, for about 30 minutes.

3. Purée the soup with a hand blender until fine and smooth. Season with salt and pepper. Optionally, you can enhance the soup with a little vegan cream. Before serving, whisk the soup with a hand blender until frothy.

Tip: When washing, bend the leaves away from each other because there is often grit and soil between them.

BITTER SALAD WITH APPLE AND JUNIPER VINAIGRETTE

Salades Amères avec Vinaigrette aux Pommes et Baies de Genièvre

TIME REQUIRED:
15 minutes + 15 minutes resting time

1 apple
2 tsp sugar
125 ml apple juice
30 ml apple cider vinegar
1 small sprig rosemary
10 juniper berries
2 heads chicory
1 head radicchio
½ head curly endive
3 tbsp olive oil
Salt
Pepper

1. Halve the apple and cut into thin wedges. Layer the apple wedges in a jar with a screw top lid.

2. Melt the sugar in a small pan to a light caramel (remember to stir!) and add the apple juice and vinegar. Bring to the boil and then simmer gently for about 5 minutes. Pour the liquid over the apple wedges, add the rosemary sprig and juniper berries, and close tightly. Leave to stand for 1 day.

3. Wash the chicory, radicchio and endive and divide the leaves into bite-sized pieces.

4. Arrange the leaves on plates. Spread apple slices over the top. Remove the rosemary sprig and juniper berries.

5. Make a vinaigrette with the apple cider vinegar and oil. Season with salt and pepper.

6. Drizzle the vinaigrette evenly over the salad.

TOMATO SORBET WITH BASIL

Sorbet de Tomate et Basilic

TIME REQUIRED:
5 minutes + 5 minutes cooling time

500 ml passata
1 tbsp tomato purée
1 tbsp lemon juice
1 pinch sugar
Salt
Pepper
Basil leaves for decoration

Tomatoes were long known as 'love apples'. It wasn't until the nineteenth century that the word 'tomato', derived from the Aztec *xitomatl*, came into common use. The Mayans had been cultivating the red fruit as early as 200 BC.

1. Mix the passata with the tomato purée, lemon juice and sugar. Season with pepper.
2. Transfer the sorbet mixture to a freezer-safe container and put it into the freezer.
3. After 4 hours, loosen the mixture with a fork and repeat the operation every half hour until it's completely frozen and the texture of snow, when it's ready to serve.
4. Use an ice-cream scoop to serve the sorbet in glasses and decorate with basil leaves. Serve immediately.

MAIN COURSES

Tomato and cashew cream tart   page 58
Pissaladière - Provençal pizza   page 60
Caramelised plum tart with Provençal pesto   page 62
Sauerkraut tart   page 64
Spinach, chickpea and hazelnut omelette   page 66
Mushroom and grape tartlets   page 68
Baked asparagus with herb sauce and duchess potatoes   page 70
Red bean and mushroom pie   page 72
Lentil and pumpkin stew   page 74
Breaded mushrooms with mustard sauce   page 76
Baguette and vegetable gratin   page 78
Provence-style lentils with cashew cheese   page 80
Stuffed artichokes cooked in red wine   page 82
Porcini mushrooms with walnuts and cranberry vinaigrette   page 84
Aubergine and lemon gratin   page 86
Gratin dauphinois   page 88
Cauliflower soufflé pie   page 90
Stuffed spinach with potato and almond balls   page 92
Ratatouille with roasted potato slices   page 94
Braised fennel with champagne sauce   page 96
Red cabbage stew   page 98
Crêpes with Cointreau cream and oranges   page 100
Courgette quiche   page 102
Coffee crêpe with almonds   page 104
Cheese crêpes with walnuts and shallots braised in red wine   page 106
Pumpkin omelette with cream sauce   page 108
Carrot, celeriac and pear tarte tatin   page 110
Quiche provençale   page 112
Crêpes with ganache and caramelised melon   page 114

TOMATO AND CASHEW CREAM TART

Tarte aux Tomates et Crème de Cajou

TIME REQUIRED: *1 hour 30 minutes*

For the base:
275 g plain flour
160 g high-quality vegan margarine, chilled
1 pinch salt
3–4 tbsp white wine (chilled)

For the filling:
200 g cashew nuts, soaked in water overnight
1 tbsp lemon juice
4 tbsp vegan cream
1 tbsp cornflour
2 tbsp yeast flakes
3 cloves garlic, chopped
Fleur de sel (or sea salt)
Pepper
1 handful basil leaves
4 tbsp marjoram
About 800 g tomatoes, assorted varieties
2 tbsp olive oil
Salt, pepper
Vegan cream, for glazing
Sprigs of herbs, to garnish

1. For the pastry, sift the flour, add the salt. Cut the chilled margarine into small pieces and add them to the flour. Quickly knead with the wine into a smooth dough (you may need to add more wine). Wrap the pastry in cling film and rest in the refrigerator for about 40 minutes.

2. In the meantime, finely grind the cashews with a hand-held blender. Mix in the lemon juice, vegan cream, cornflour, yeast flakes and chopped garlic. Season with a little fleur de sel and pepper.

3. Preheat the oven to 200°C/400°F/gas 6. Line a baking tray with baking parchment. On a floured pastry board, roll out the pastry to a 3-mm thickness and shape into a 25 x 40-cm rectangle. Place the pastry on a baking tray. Prick evenly with a fork several times, and leave a 2-cm-wide margin on all sides. Refrigerate for 20 more minutes.

4. Spread the cashew cream over the pastry, leaving the margins free. Wash and slice the tomatoes. Chop the herbs. Spread the tomatoes out in a thick layer over the cream and season with salt and pepper. Turn up the edges and brush with vegan cream.

5. Bake on the middle shelf for 20 minutes. Then sprinkle with the chopped herbs and bake for 20–25 more minutes, until done. Garnish with sprigs of herbs and serve.

PROVENÇAL PIZZA

Pissaladière

TIME REQUIRED: *2 hours 30 minutes*

For the pastry base:
500 g flour
1½ sachets dry yeast
1 tsp salt
1 pinch sugar
2 tbsp olive oil
About 250 ml lukewarm water

For the topping:
1.5 kg onions
4 tbsp olive oil
2 tbsp high-quality vegan margarine
2 bay leaves
1 tsp dried thyme
1 tsp dried savory
Salt, pepper

2 tbsp currants
25 pitted black olives
1 tbsp olive oil
Pepper

Pissaladière is Italian pizza's sister from Provence.

1. Sift the flour, yeast, salt and sugar into a bowl. Add a tablespoon of oil to the water and knead with the flour mixture to form a smooth and elastic dough. Knead well until the surface turns glossy. Roll the dough into a ball and rub with the remaining tablespoon of oil. Put it into a bowl and cover with a cloth. Leave the dough to rise in a warm place for 1–1½ hours, until it doubles in size. Then knead it again well, cover and rest for 30 more minutes.

2. In the meantime, make the onion confit. Peel and slice the onions into about 4-mm-thick rings. Preheat the oven to 180°C/350°F/gas 4.

3. Melt the margarine in a medium-sized shallow ovenproof dish. Spread out half the onion rings in the dish, crumble over the bay leaves and sprinkle with half the thyme and savory. Season with pepper and salt, drizzle with 2 tablespoons of olive oil and cover with the remaining onion rings. There should be a 3-cm-thick layer of onions, otherwise you may need a smaller dish. Sprinkle with the remaining herbs and oil and put the dish into the oven (middle shelf). Cook the onion rings for 60–80 minutes, stirring them every 10 minutes. The confit is ready when the onions turn golden brown and with a melting consistency.

4. Preheat the oven to 240°C/475°F/gas 9 and insert a baking tray into the top third.

5. On a floured pastry board, knead the dough well and then roll it out into a rectangle. Lay the dough on a sheet of baking parchment. Press around the dough to leave a slightly higher edge. Spread the onion confit over the dough and scatter the olives and currants over the top. Lay the pissaladière with the baking parchment on the hot tray in the oven and bake for 12–15 minutes. Take it out of the oven, drizzle with a tablespoon of olive oil and season with freshly ground pepper.

CARAMELISED PLUM TART WITH PROVENÇAL PESTO

Tarte aux Prunes Caramélisées et Pesto Provençal

TIME REQUIRED: *1 hour*

2 tart moulds (18 cm in diameter)

For the base:
2 packets vegan spelt puff pastry

For the filling:
500 g soya yoghurt (300 g drained)
300 g prune plums
1 onion
1 tbsp olive oil
1 tbsp sugar
1 tbsp red wine vinegar
100 ml red wine
Salt, pepper
2 cloves garlic, chopped
150 g grated vegan cheese
2 tbsp cornflour
Salt, pepper
3–4 sprigs thyme
2 tbsp dry breadcrumbs

Provençal pesto (see recipe on page 26)

PRUNE PLUMS ARE purplish blue with somewhat pointed ends, while round plums can be purple, red, yellow and green.

1. Put the soya yoghurt into a cotton cloth or a coffee filter and leave to drain overnight.

2. Make the pesto according to the recipe and set aside in the refrigerator.

3. Wash the plums and set 8 of them aside. De-stone and coarsely dice the remainder. Peel and cut the onion into thin rings. Heat the olive oil in a pan, sprinkle in the sugar and cook to a caramel. Add the diced plums and onion rings and stir well. Deglaze the pan with the vinegar and wine, turn down the heat and simmer everything for 20 minutes. Season with salt, pepper and chopped garlic. Leave to cool. Mix the drained yoghurt well with the grated cheese and cornflour, and season with salt and pepper.

4. Line the two tart moulds (18 cm in diameter) with puff pastry. To do this, spread out the pastry, place one of the moulds over it and cut out a disc that is a little larger than the mould. Press the pastry inside the moulds and up the sides, and trim off any excess. Prick the base several times with a fork. Sprinkle a tablespoon of breadcrumbs over each tart base and brush each one with half the yoghurt. Spread the caramelised plums over the top and sprinkle with thyme. Blanch the plums that were set aside in hot water. Then peel and de-stone them and arrange them on the tarts.

5. Bake the tarts in the oven preheated to 200°C/400°F/gas 6 on the middle shelf for 15–20 minutes, until golden. Cut both tarts in half and serve with Provençal pesto.

SAUERKRAUT TART

Tarte à la Choucroute

TIME REQUIRED: *2 hours*

Tart mould
 (24 cm in diameter)

For the filling:
500 g sauerkraut
10 juniper berries
1 tsp caraway seeds
3 bay leaves
1 onion
4 cloves garlic
2–3 tbsp oil
1 tbsp plain flour
Salt, pepper
450 g tinned haricot
 beans
1 large sour apple
250 g waxy potatoes
1 tsp fresh savory (or 1 tsp
 dried)

For the base:
1 packet vegan puff pastry

Dried beans or rice, for
 blind baking
Olive oil, for drizzling

In addition to its naturopathic benefits, sauerkraut can be used to make delicious dishes.

1. Combine the sauerkraut, juniper berries, caraway seeds and bay leaves in a large pan, cover with water and bring to the boil. Turn down the heat and simmer for 20 minutes, adding water if necessary. Take care not to let the sauerkraut burn.

2. Peel and finely slice the onion and garlic. Heat the oil in a frying pan and sauté the onion and garlic until translucent and stir in the flour until everything turns light brown. Add the sauerkraut, stir well and add a little more water. Wash and coarsely dice the potatoes and apple. Add them to the sauerkraut. Add a little more water, stir and simmer for 10–15 minutes. Mix in the beans and savory. Season with salt and pepper.

3. Line a large tart mould (24 cm in diameter) with the puff pastry, pressing firmly. Line the pastry with baking parchment and cover to a height of 1 cm with dried beans or rice. Bake in the oven preheated to 180°C/350°F/gas 4 for 15 minutes. Take out the beans or rice (they can be used for another purpose) and bake for 10 more minutes, until the pastry turns crispy.

4. Take the tart base out of the oven and fill with the sauerkraut and bean mixture. Bake for 15 minutes more, and then for 5 more minutes under the grill. Drizzle the tart with olive oil and leave to cool a little. Cut it into quarters and serve.

SPINACH, CHICKPEA AND HAZELNUT OMELETTE

Omelette aux Épinards, Pois Chiches et Noisettes

TIME REQUIRED:
40 minutes

400 g tinned chickpeas
80 g hazelnuts
2 shallots
4 cloves garlic
6 tbsp olive oil
200 g tomatoes
300 g spinach
2 tbsp plain flour
2 tbsp dry breadcrumbs
Salt, pepper
2 tbsp dried basil
4 cherry tomatoes

Hazelnuts are mainly grown in the Savoy and south-western regions of France.

1. Pour the chickpeas into a sieve, then rinse and drain.
2. Coarsely chop the hazelnuts and peel and dice the shallots and garlic. Heat a tablespoon of olive oil in a frying pan and sauté the shallots and garlic until golden. Add the tomatoes, diced, and spinach and sauté together for 5 minutes.
3. Combine the chickpeas and hazelnuts with a tablespoon of olive oil in a blending beaker and grind to a paste with a hand-held blender. Mix with the sautéed vegetables in a bowl and incorporate the flour and breadcrumbs. Finally, season generously with salt, pepper and basil.
4. Heat a tablespoon of olive oil in a non-stick frying pan and half the omelette mixture. Spread it evenly inside the pan and fry gently. When the bottom of the omelette is golden and crispy, transfer to a plate. Heat another tablespoon of olive oil in the pan and add 2 cherry tomatoes, sliced. Return the omelette to the pan with the crispy side facing upwards. Fry until done, then keep warm in the oven. Repeat the process with the remaining half of the omelette mixture. Halve each omelette and serve.

MUSHROOM AND GRAPE TARTLETS

Tartelettes aux Champignons et Raisins

TIME REQUIRED:
30 minutes

8 tartlet moulds (8 cm in diameter)

For the base:
1 packet vegan spelt puff pastry

For the filling:
8 tsp Dijon mustard (or wholegrain mustard)
8–12 button mushrooms, sliced
150 g grapes
8 tbsp grated vegan cheese
Fleur de sel
Pepper
Olive oil, for drizzling
4 sprigs rosemary

1. Preheat the oven to 200°C /400°F/gas 6.

2. Roll out the pastry, place the tartlet moulds over it and cut out pastry discs. Carefully line the moulds with the pastry and prick with a fork.

3. Spread the pastry with mustard, fill with mushrooms and grapes, and sprinkle with grated cheese. Season with fleur de sel and pepper, and drizzle with a little olive oil.

4. Place the moulds in the oven and bake for about 20 minutes (top with half a rosemary sprig after 10 minutes).

Tip: Fresh button mushrooms have tightly closed caps, while open gills show that they have been stored for some time.

BAKED ASPARAGUS WITH HERB SAUCE AND DUCHESS POTATOES

Asperges au Four sur Miroir aux Herbes avec Pommes Duchesse

TIME REQUIRED:
45 minutes

For the baked asparagus:
16 asparagus spears
1.5 litres water
Juice of ½ lemon
1 tsp salt
1 pinch sugar
4 cloves garlic
2 handfuls spinach
1 packet strudel dough
50 g margarine, melted

For the duchess potatoes:
500 g potatoes
50 g vegan margarine, melted
2 tbsp plain flour
1 tsp salt

For the sauce:
250 g root vegetables (carrots, parsley roots and celeriac)
50 g leek

Asparagus contains folic acid, magnesium, vitamin B, vitamin E, dietary fibre and a large number of bioactive compounds.

1. Combine the water, lemon juice, salt and sugar in a deep pan and bring to the boil. Cook the asparagus until firm to the bite. Refresh in cold water and dry on kitchen paper.
2. Peel the garlic cloves, crush them through a garlic press and lightly season with salt. Wash and dry the spinach.
3. Cut the strudel dough into 15 x 15-cm squares and lay it out. Wrap the asparagus in the spinach leaves with the garlic paste and lay them on the dough squares. Wrap the spears in the dough, leaving the tips uncovered. Paint the dough with the melted margarine.
4. Boil the potatoes in salted water until soft, then peel and mash through a potato ricer. Leave to cool.
5. Mix the mashed potato with the melted margarine, flour and salt, and knead into a dough. Transfer to a piping bag (large nozzle) and pipe swirls over a baking tray lined with baking parchment.

MAIN COURSES

3 spring onions
1 tbsp olive oil
250 ml water (or white wine)
100 ml passata
1 tbsp dried herbs (oregano, thyme, rosemary)
Salt
Pepper

6. Lay the asparagus parcels on another lined baking tray (one tray may be enough).

7. Preheat the oven to 180°C/350°F/gas 4 and insert both trays. The edges of the duchess potatoes should be lightly browned, while the baked asparagus should turn a golden brown colour.

8. For the sauce, finely dice the root vegetables, leek and spring onions, and fry in olive oil until light brown. Add the water (or wine) and braise for about 10 minutes. Add the passata and dried herbs, and simmer for 5 more minutes. Strain the sauce and season with salt and pepper.

RED BEAN AND MUSHROOM PIE

Paté aux Haricots et Champignons

TIME REQUIRED: *1 hour 30 minutes + resting time*

Pie tin (18 cm in diameter)

For the shortcrust pastry:
250 g wheat or spelt flour
½ tsp salt
150 g high-quality vegan margarine, cold
4 tbsp iced water
Or 1 packet (300 g) vegan shortcrust pastry

For the filling:
400 g tin red kidney beans (255 g drained weight)
150 g button mushrooms
1 onion
3 tbsp cornflour or arrowroot
4 tbsp white wine
150 ml oat cream
2 tbsp chopped parsley

Pies are made by encasing an exquisitely seasoned filling in pastry. The *farce*, as the filling is known in French, is a mixture of finely chopped, well-seasoned ingredients that are bound together with cream or béchamel sauce. Pies can be filled with a stew.

Pies are made with a special unsweetened shortcrust pastry or puff pastry. An ovenproof dish or pie tin is lined with a thin layer of pastry and filled with the *farce*. This is then covered with a tightly sealed pastry lid, into which one or more holes is made to allow the steam to escape.

1. For the pastry, mix the flour and salt in a bowl. Use a knife to cut pieces of the cold margarine into the flour and rub them in with your fingers until crumbs form. Work in the iced water with a fork, then quickly knead the dough. Roll the dough into a ball, wrap in cling film and refrigerate for 1 hour.

2. In the meantime, drain the beans. Trim and slice the mushrooms. Peel and chop the onion. Mix the cornflour or arrowroot with the wine. Bring the oat cream to the boil and dissolve the wine and starch mixture. Boil for 2 minutes while stirring constantly. Mix the beans, mushrooms and onion into the oat cream mixture.

3. Roll out the dough over a floured work surface. Lay the pie mould on top of the pastry and cut out a disc of the same diameter. Grease the pie mould with oil and flour and line the bottom with the pastry. Knead the remainder of the pastry and roll it out again. Cut out another 18-cm-diameter disc and set it

1 tsp salt
Pepper
Oil and flour, for greasing
Soya cream, for glazing

aside. Use the rest of the pastry to make the sides of the pie and add to the mould (join well with the base).

4. Pre-heat the oven to 180°C/350°F/gas 4. Carefully fill the pie with the bean mixture and cover with the pastry disc (seal well around the edges). Cut the remaining pastry into the shape of leaves and small balls to decorate the pie. Cut out a small circular hole in the middle of the lid and insert a 'chimney' (a metal piping nozzle can be used for this purpose). This will allow moisture to be drawn from the filling and evaporate in the form of steam as the pie bakes. Brush with a little soya cream. Bake on the middle shelf for 45–50 minutes, until the lid turns a lovely golden brown.

LENTIL AND PUMPKIN STEW

Ragoût de Lentilles et Citrouille

TIME REQUIRED: *1 hour*

500 g pumpkin or red kuri squash
3 tbsp olive oil
250 g shallots
4 cloves garlic
6 tbsp olive oil
350 g tomatoes
1 litre vegetable broth (made from 500 ml vegetable stock, see recipe on page 22)
300 g brown lentils, dried
3 bay leaves
1 tsp dried oregano
1 bunch parsley, chopped
1 pinch ground nutmeg
1 tbsp red wine vinegar
Salt, pepper
200 g vegan crème fraîche
Sprigs of thyme and of oregano

Lentils are native to Asia and are among the earliest plants to be cultivated.

1. Wash, halve and de-seed the squash. Preheat the oven to 200°C/400°F/gas 6. Cut the squash into 3–4-cm pieces. Put the squash pieces on a baking tray lined with baking parchment and drizzle with 3 tablespoons of olive oil. Roast the squash on the middle shelf for 20 minutes, turning the pieces over often, until soft. Take them out of the oven.

2. Peel and thinly slice the shallots and garlic. Heat the remaining oil in a large pan and sauté the shallots and garlic until golden. Score the tomatoes with a cross and pour boiling water over them. Peel and coarsely dice. Add the diced tomato to the shallots and sauté quickly. Pour in the vegetable broth and add the lentils, bay leaves and oregano. Bring to the boil. Turn down the heat and simmer for 40 minutes (the lentils should be soft). Remove the bay leaves.

3. Add the squash to the lentils and lightly purée with a hand-held blender in short bursts. Season well with the chopped parsley, nutmeg, vinegar, salt and pepper. Garnish the lentils with the crème fraîche, squash pieces and herbs.

BREADED MUSHROOMS WITH MUSTARD SAUCE

Champignons de Paris Panés à la Sauce Moutarde

TIME REQUIRED:
45 minutes

For the mushrooms:
400 g button mushrooms
50 g plain flour
250 ml soda water
2 tbsp chickpea flour
50 g dry breadcrumbs
Salt
Oil, for deep-frying

For the mustard sauce:
1 small onion
6 sweet-and-sour gherkins
2 tsp Dijon mustard
250 ml vegan cream
1 tbsp apple cider vinegar
1 tbsp olive oil
Salt, pepper

HALF OF THE mustard produced in France comes from Dijon, in Burgundy. Ground black and brown mustard seeds are combined with the juice of ripe grapes to give the typical piquant, tart and yet mild flavour.

1. Clean the mushrooms with a brush and trim off the stems. Halve or quarter the larger mushrooms. Season with salt. Prepare 3 plates, one with the flour, another with a batter made by whisking the chickpea flour with the soda water, and the last with the breadcrumbs. Dust the mushrooms with flour, then dip in the batter and coat with breadcrumbs.

2. Heat the oil in a frying pan. Add the mushrooms, turn down the heat a little and fry until golden, turning often. Drain the excess oil on kitchen paper.

3. For the mustard sauce, finely chop the onion and dice the gherkins. Heat the olive oil in a small saucepan and lightly sauté the onion. Mix the vegan cream with the mustard, diced gherkin and vinegar. Stir the mixture into the onion. Simmer for a couple of minutes and season with salt and pepper. Serve with the breaded mushrooms.

BAGUETTE AND VEGETABLE GRATIN

Gratin de Baguette et Légumes au Vin Blanc

TIME REQUIRED:
40 minutes

120 g spring onions
180 g leeks
250 g broccoli
1 tbsp high-quality vegan margarine
3 cloves garlic
2 tbsp olive oil
8 sage leaves
2 tbsp chopped parsley
About 200 g baguette (see recipe on page 14)
75 ml white wine
200 ml vegetable stock (see recipe on page 22)
180 g grated vegan cheese
Salt, pepper
1 tbsp vegan margarine, for greasing

THE FIRST BAGUETTE in Paris is said to have been baked by an Austrian who emigrated to France after the Congress of Vienna.

1. Wash and trim the spring onions and leeks, and slice them into rings. Cut the broccoli into florets and wash them. Cook them with 1 tablespoon of margarine over low heat for 10 minutes. Peel and chop the garlic.

2. Heat the oil in a frying pan and sauté the garlic, leeks and spring onions. Turn down the heat and cook until still firm to the bite. Add the broccoli and season with salt and pepper. Chop and stir in the sage and chopped parsley. Set aside 1 tablespoon of the mixed herbs for the garnish.

3. Preheat the oven to 200°C/400°F/gas 6. Grease an ovenproof dish by brushing with margarine. Cut the bread into about 2-cm-thick slices and fill the dish. Distribute the vegetables evenly over the top. Combine the vegetable stock (it need not be homemade) and wine, bring to the boil and pour over the bread and vegetables. Sprinkle over with grated vegan cheese and bake on the middle shelf for about 25 minutes, until golden brown.

4. Sprinkle with the rest of the herbs.

MAIN COURSES

PROVENCE-STYLE LENTILS WITH CASHEW CHEESE

Lentilles à la Provençale au Fromage de Cajou

TIME REQUIRED:
30 minutes

For the lentils:
1 kg lentils
8 cherry tomatoes
1 small courgette, sliced
1 small aubergine, diced
6 small button mushrooms
4 olives
3 cloves garlic
2 tbsp olive oil
1 tsp dried Herbes de Provence (optional)
3 tbsp olive oil
4 tbsp white wine vinegar
1 tbsp fresh thyme leaves
Salt

For the cashew cheese:
100 g cashew nuts, soaked overnight
2 tbsp yeast flakes
1 tsp lemon juice
100 g tinned haricot beans
Salt, pepper
125 ml water

LENTILS ARE GRADED according to size and the smallest are often considered to have the most flavour. The red variety are cooked the fastest. They contain little sodium (salt), but plenty of potassium, phosphorous and iron.

1. Wash the lentils and cook according to the instructions on the packet. Strain, stir with a fork and leave to cool.

2. Line a baking tray with baking parchment and preheat the oven to 200°C/400°F/gas 6.

3. Put the tomatoes, courgette, aubergine, and mushrooms on the tray and drizzle with the 2 tablespoons of olive oil. Roast them in the oven until light golden and leave to cool.

4. Mix the lentils with the roasted vegetables and add the olives and chopped garlic.

5. Make a dressing with the Herbes de Provence, oil, vinegar, salt and pepper and pour it over the lentils. Leave to stand for about 3 hours.

6. For the cashew cheese, rinse the cashews in cold water and leave to drain.

7. Combine the cashews, yeast flakes, lemon juice and beans, and season with salt and pepper. Add 125 ml of water and purée with a hand-held blender.

8. Put the purée into a small saucepan over a medium heat and stir until it acquires the consistency of cheese. Leave to cool.

9. Fill small jars with the lentils and cashew cheese or arrange on plates. Garnish with thyme.

STUFFED ARTICHOKES COOKED IN RED WINE

Artichauts Farcis au Vin Rouge

TIME REQUIRED: *1 hour 30 minutes*

4 artichokes
1 tbsp lemon juice
2 cloves garlic
1 shallot
1 pepper
1 tbsp capers
2 tbsp chopped basil
5 tbsp olive oil
2 tbsp dry breadcrumbs
Salt, pepper
1 untreated lemon
2 small pears
10 pitted olives
250 ml red wine

The artichokes grown in Normandy, with their tightly packed purplish and pointed leaves, are more delicate than the ones grown in Brittany.

1. Trim the artichoke stems to a length of 3 cm and peel them with a vegetable peeler. Halve the artichokes across the middle and break off tough outer leaves. Scoop out the choke and thin inner leaves with a sharp spoon. Mix 2 litres of water with the lemon juice and soak the prepared artichokes.

2. Peel and finely dice the garlic and shallot. Wash, de-seed and dice the pepper. Chop the capers and mix together with the chopped basil. Mix them with 3 tablespoons of olive oil and the breadcrumbs. Season with salt and pepper.

3. Preheat the oven to 200°C/400°F/gas 6. Stuff the artichokes with the vegetable mixture, packing firmly. Arrange the artichokes, stem-side facing upwards, in an ovenproof frying pan.

4. Rinse and cut the lemon into wedges and halve the pears. Add them with the olives to the artichokes. Drizzle the artichokes with 2 tablespoons of olive oil and add the wine. Cover the pan with aluminium foil, place on the middle shelf and cook for about 60 minutes. Remove the foil and roast for 10 more minutes, until the artichokes turn a lovely colour.

PORCINI MUSHROOMS WITH WALNUTS AND CRANBERRY VINAIGRETTE

Bolets aux Noix et Vinaigrette aux Canneberges

TIME REQUIRED: *1 hour*

1 tsp sugar
100 ml apple cider vinegar
100 ml apple juice
1 tbsp cranberry jam
4 tbsp hazelnut oil (or other vegetable oil)
4 tbsp corn oil
300 g porcini mushrooms (or a different variety, e.g. Portobello mushrooms)
4 handfuls lamb's lettuce
2 cloves garlic
2 tbsp olive oil
50 g walnuts
12 slices baguette (see recipe on page 14)
3 sprigs thyme
Salt, pepper

Vinaigrette is a sauce whose main ingredients are vinegar and oil.

1. For the vinaigrette, melt the sugar in a pan and add the vinegar and apple juice. Stir briskly with a whisk, turn down the heat and simmer for 5 minutes. Mix the jam with the vinegar mixture and leave to stand for 1 hour. Stir in the hazelnut and corn oils, and season with salt and pepper.
2. Cut off the base of the mushrooms and clean them with a brush. Slice them lengthways.
3. Wash and shake dry the lamb's lettuce.
4. Peel and thinly slice the garlic.
5. Heat the olive oil in a frying pan and sauté the mushroom slices on both sides. Season lightly with salt and pepper. Add and sauté the garlic. Pluck the thyme.
6. Dress the lamb's lettuce with the vinaigrette and arrange on plates with the mushrooms, walnuts and baguette slices. Sprinkle over with thyme leaves.

Tip: Cranberries, with their bitter and slightly tart flavour, are easy to make into a delicious jam.

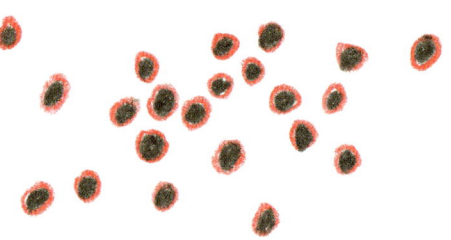

AUBERGINE AND LEMON GRATIN

Aubergines Gratinées au Citron

TIME REQUIRED:
40 minutes

8 small aubergines
1 lemon
6 cloves garlic
6 cherry tomatoes
6 tbsp chopped fresh parsley
2 tbsp chopped fresh basil
200 g coarse dry breadcrumbs
2 tsp dried thyme
Salt, pepper
Olive oil (as needed)

1. Preheat the oven to 220°C/425°F/gas 7. Wash and halve the aubergines. Use a spoon to carefully scoop out the flesh, leaving a 5-mm border. Set aside the flesh. Squeeze the lemon. Rub the aubergine halves with the juice.

2. Peel and chop the garlic. Score the tomatoes with a cross, pour boiling water over them and peel. Dice the aubergine flesh and tomatoes.

3. Mix the aubergine and tomato mixture well with the chopped garlic, parsley, basil and breadcrumbs and season with thyme, salt and pepper. Knead the mixture, adding enough olive oil to bind everything together.

4. Pack the aubergine halves with the filling and place them on a baking tray lined with baking parchment. Place the tray on the middle shelf and bake for 10–15 minutes, until crispy.

Tip: When you press on a fresh aubergine with your finger, the skin should spring back, otherwise the flesh has already turned spongy.

GRATIN DAUPHINOIS

Gratin de Pommes de Terre

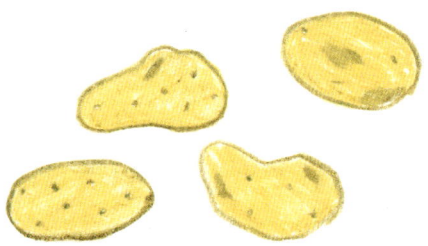

TIME REQUIRED:
80 minutes

1 kg waxy potatoes
6 tbsp high-quality vegan margarine
150 g grated vegan cheese
Scant 1 tsp freshly grated nutmeg
2 tsp salt
Pepper
250 ml soya milk

This classic potato dish hails from the historical French region of Dauphiné.

1. Peel the potatoes and cut them into 2-mm-thick slices. Grease a shallow ovenproof dish with 2 tablespoons of margarine. Arrange half the potato slices in a layer in the dish. Sprinkle them with 1 teaspoon of salt, half the grated cheese and half the nutmeg. Distribute 2 tablespoons of margarine in small pieces over the top. Make another layer with the remaining potato slices, season with salt, pepper and nutmeg, and sprinkle with the rest of the cheese. Distribute the rest of the margarine over the top. Carefully pour over the soya milk and gently tilt the dish back and forth.
2. Preheat the oven to 220°C/425°F/gas 7. Bake on the middle shelf for about 45 minutes. The milk should be absorbed by the potatoes and the top layer should develop a golden brown crust. Serve immediately.

Tip: Never use floury potatoes to make a gratin! Also, the slices should be cut as thinly as possible.

CAULIFLOWER SOUFFLÉ PIE

Soufflé de Chou-Fleur en Croûte Feuilletée

TIME REQUIRED: *1 hour*

600 g cauliflower
50 g pine nuts
3 cloves garlic
200 g silken tofu
1 large bunch parsley, chopped
100 g sandwich bread, crust removed
3 tbsp olive oil
1 tbsp cornflour
½ packet vegan puff pastry
2 tbsp coarse dry breadcrumbs
Salt, pepper
Oil, for greasing
Dried beans, for blind baking

1 tbsp apple cider vinegar

Soufflé literally means 'puffed' and is used to describe light and airy casseroles, although the word casserole is perhaps unsuitable as it tends to be a somewhat heavier dish. Soufflés can be adapted as starters, main courses and desserts.

1. Preheat the oven to 200°C/400°F/gas 6.
2. Trim and cut the cauliflower into florets. Wash and cook the florets until firm to the bite. Leave to drain in a sieve, transfer to a blending beaker and purée with a hand-held blender.
3. Chop the pine nuts and peel and slice the garlic. Add the tofu, pine nuts, garlic and parsley to the puréed cauliflower. Crumble in the bread and add together with 1 tablespoon of olive oil and the cornflour. Mix well. Season with salt and pepper.
4. Grease an ovenproof dish with oil. Fully line the dish with the puff pastry, pressing firmly. Cover the pastry with baking parchment and fill it with the beans. Blind bake the pastry on the middle shelf for 10 minutes. Remove the beans and parchment and fill with the cauliflower mixture. Sprinkle over with the breadcrumbs and drizzle with a little olive oil. Bake for about 45 minutes.

Tip: You can also omit the puff pastry and bake cauliflower soufflés in 4 small ramekins. The baking time will be shorter. The soufflés should be soft on the inside and golden brown on the outside.

STUFFED SPINACH WITH POTATO AND ALMOND BALLS

Feuilles d'Épinards Farcies et Pommes de Terre aux Amandes

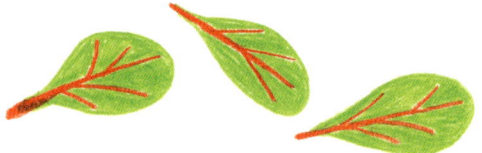

TIME REQUIRED: *1 hour*

For the stuffed spinach:
500 g large spinach leaves
350 g button mushrooms
2 shallots
3 cloves garlic
2 tbsp sunflower oil
50 g pine nuts
50 g sandwich bread, crust removed
150 ml vegan cream
1 tsp cornflour
1 pinch nutmeg
Salt, pepper

For the potato and almond balls:
500 g floury potatoes
50 g vegan margarine
2 tbsp plant-based milk
1 tsp cornflour
100 g flaked almonds
Salt

A DISTINCTION IS made between summer and autumn spinach, which has soft leaves, and winter spinach, with its thicker and aromatic leaves, which is picked in March.

1. Trim and wash the spinach leaves, removing the thicker stems, and blanch for about 5 minutes in salted water. Refresh the leaves in an ice bath and spread them out over cloths to dry.

2. Trim and thinly slice the mushrooms. Peel and finely chop the shallots and garlic. Heat the oil and sauté the shallots, garlic and pine nuts. Add the mushrooms and sauté together. When everything is golden brown, crumble in the bread and mix. Season with salt and pepper.

3. Preheat the oven to 200°C/400°F/gas 6. Assemble the spinach leaves to make eight 12 x 14-cm rectangles. Spread about 2 tablespoons of the filling in the middle of each rectangle, fold in the sides and roll them up. Grease a baking tray with oil and arrange the spinach rolls inside. Mix the vegan cream with cornflour and season with nutmeg, salt and pepper. Pour it evenly over the spinach rolls. Bake in the oven for 15–20 minutes.

4. Wash and cook the potatoes in salted water until firm to the bite. Drain and peel. Mash the potatoes through a ricer and then mix well with the cornflour, plant-based milk, margarine and salt. Shape the mixture into balls with your hands.

5. Toast the flaked almonds in a dry, non-stick frying pan until golden brown and coat the balls with them. Serve together with the spinach rolls.

RATATOUILLE WITH ROASTED POTATO SLICES

Ratatouille et Rondelles de Pommes de Terre Frites

TIME REQUIRED:
45 minutes

For the potato slices:
500 g waxy potatoes
2 tbsp olive oil
Salt

For the ratatouille:
300 g aubergines
200 g courgettes
300 g red and green peppers
500 g tomatoes
250 g red onions
4 cloves garlic
1 sprig thyme
1 small sprig rosemary
1 sage leaf
1 sprig savory
Salt, pepper

A traditional summer dish from Provence with the region's characteristic herbs – thyme, sage, rosemary and savory. This dish can be enjoyed both hot and cold.

1. Preheat the oven to 200°C/400°F/gas 6. Wash, peel and cut the potatoes into about 3-mm-thick slices. Line a baking tray with baking parchment and spread out the potato slices over the tray. Drizzle with olive oil and roast in the oven until crispy and golden (about 35 minutes).

2. Wash, dry and cut the vegetables into about 2-cm dice. Peel and finely dice the garlic. Slice the onions into rings. Pluck the herbs, removing any stems. Optionally, cut them into smaller pieces. Heat 2 tablespoons of oil in a large frying pan. Sauté the onion rings, garlic and diced peppers one after the other. Then turn down the heat and cook until soft.

3. Add the diced tomatoes and herbs, season with salt and pepper and cook for 25 more minutes.

4. Heat the remaining oil in a second frying pan and sauté the diced courgettes and aubergines. Turn the heat down to low and cook for 15 minutes. Add the contents of this pan to that of the first pan and cook together for 5 minutes. Season with salt and pepper.

5. Season the potato slices with salt and serve with the ratatouille.

BRAISED FENNEL WITH CHAMPAGNE SAUCE

Fenouil Braisé et Sauce au Champagne

TIME REQUIRED:
30 minutes + cooking time

For the braised fennel:
3 fennel bulbs
1 apple (e.g. Granny Smith)
2 tbsp olive oil
200 g tomatoes
1 tbsp capers
1 tsp thyme leaves (1 sprig)
2 tbsp vegan margarine
40 g coarse dry breadcrumbs
2 tbsp chopped parsley
2 tbsp oregano leaves
Salt, ground nutmeg, pepper
Oil, for greasing

For the champagne sauce:
1 shallot
300 ml champagne (or sparkling wine)

Capers are the flower buds of the caper bushes that grow in the south of France. They're preserved in vinegar or brine and are used to enhance many dishes.

1. Preheat the oven to 220°C/425°F/gas 7.

2. Trim and wash the fennel, removing the fronds. Halve the bulbs lengthways and cut lengthways into about 1-cm-wide slices. Wash, halve and core the apple and cut into 1-cm-wide wedges.

3. Heat the oil in a large frying pan. Sauté the fennel and apple, stirring gently, until golden brown.

4. Wash the tomatoes, then score them with a cross and pour boiling water over them in a bowl. Refresh in cold water and peel. Dice the tomatoes and add with the chopped capers to the vegetables in the pan. Sprinkle over with thyme and cook briefly until the tomatoes start to fall apart. Cover the pan and cook over a low heat for 5 minutes. Then remove the lid and cook for 10 more minutes, until the tomatoes are concentrated. Season with nutmeg, salt and pepper.

5. Grease an ovenproof dish with oil. Fill the dish with the fruit and vegetable mixture. Cover with an even layer of breadcrumbs, distribute small pieces of margarine evenly over the top and sprinkle with the oregano. Bake for 15–20 minutes. Sprinkle with fresh parsley before serving.

6. For the champagne sauce, peel and finely chop the shallot. Combine with the champagne in a pan, place over the heat and

*200 ml vegetable stock
 (see recipe on page 22)*
100 ml vegan cream
80 g cold vegan margarine

Lemon juice (optional)
Salt, pepper

reduce by half. Add the vegetable stock and simmer until the liquid is reduced by two-thirds. Filter through a fine-mesh sieve, combine with the vegan cream and bring to the boil. Remove from the heat and season with salt and pepper. Before serving, stir in the cold margarine over a medium heat until the sauce thickens to a creamy consistency. Season with salt and pepper, and optionally with 1 teaspoon of lemon juice.

RED CABBAGE STEW

Ragoût de Chou Rouge

TIME REQUIRED: *1 hour*

500 ml vegetable stock (see recipe on page 22)
600 g red cabbage
600 g potatoes
250 g apples
2 tbsp lemon juice
2 tbsp olive oil
1 tbsp sugar (or maple syrup)
2 tsp caraway seeds
½ onion
5 cloves
1 bay leaf
5 juniper berries
100 ml red wine
200 g roasted chestnuts
Salt, pepper

Juniper berries have a slightly resinous flavour. The small evergreen shrub is mainly found in the alpine regions of France. They are also an important flavouring ingredient for sauerkraut.

1. Make the vegetable stock.
2. Remove the outermost (withered) leaves from the cabbage. Cut the cabbage into quarters, remove the stalks and shred each quarter into 5-mm-wide strips. Wash in a sieve and leave to drain.
3. Wash, peel and cut the potatoes into about 1-cm dice. Wash, halve, core and dice the apples.
4. Mix the cabbage strips and diced apples well with the lemon juice and work in the juice a little with your hands. Heat the olive oil in a large pan. Sauté the red cabbage and apple over a high heat, stirring constantly. Mix in the diced potatoes and sauté together, then mix in the sugar or syrup and briefly caramelise. Season with the caraway seeds, pour in the vegetable stock and stir. Stud the onion with the cloves and add together with the bay leaf and juniper berries to the pan. Cover and cook over a low heat for about 30 minutes, stirring often.
5. Add the wine and season with salt and pepper. Simmer for 5 minutes and then remove the onion and add the chestnuts. After cooking for 5 more minutes over a low heat, the cabbage should be falling apart and ready to be served. Optionally, you can add 1 tablespoon of balsamic vinegar.

CRÊPES WITH COINTREAU CREAM AND ORANGES

Crêpes à la Crème Cointreau et Oranges

TIME REQUIRED:
40 minutes

For the crêpes:
600 ml rice milk
1 pinch salt
200 g plain flour
2 tbsp apple purée
2 tbsp cornflour
Oil, for cooking

For the cream:
500 g soya yoghurt
1 tsp Cointreau
¼ tsp vanilla extract
1–2 tbsp icing sugar
2 tsp grated orange zest
200 ml soya cream, whipped
1 sachet whipped cream stabiliser

Cointreau is a liqueur made from the rinds of sweet and bitter oranges.

1. For the cream, leave the soya yoghurt to drain in a sieve overnight.
2. Mix the firm yoghurt with the Cointreau, vanilla, sugar and orange zest. Whip the soya cream with the stabiliser and fold into the yoghurt mixture. Set aside in the refrigerator.
3. For the crêpes, mix the rice milk with the remaining ingredients to a smooth batter. Rest for about 15 minutes.
4. Heat 1 tablespoon of oil in a crêpe pan (or a medium, non-stick, shallow frying pan). When the pan is very hot, pour a ladle of batter into the centre. Gently tilt the pan to spread the batter evenly. After two minutes, carefully loosen and lift up the edges of the crêpe with a spatula or palette knife. If the underside is golden brown, flip the crêpe and continue to cook until it has a nice colour all over. Slide the crêpe onto a plate and keep warm in the oven. Wipe the pan with kitchen paper after each crêpe and add a little more oil. Repeat the process until the batter is used up.
5. Fill the crêpes with Cointreau cream and serve with orange wedges or slices.

COURGETTE QUICHE

Quiche à la Courgette

TIME REQUIRED: *1 hour + 2 hours refrigeration time*

4 ramekins or small ovenproof dishes (about 12 cm in diameter)

For the shortcrust pastry:
400 g soya yoghurt (drained overnight)
170 g high-quality vegan margarine
250 g plain flour (or spelt flour, optionally)
½ tsp salt
Or 1 packet (300 g) vegan shortcrust pastry

For the filling:
300 g béchamel sauce (see recipe on page 30)
4 cloves garlic, chopped
100 g grated vegan cheese
1 handful basil, chopped

The word 'quiche' is derived from the German word *kuchen*, meaning cake. It is a French speciality that originated in the region of Lorraine.

1. Leave about 400 g of soya yoghurt to drain overnight in a sieve lined with a cotton cloth to yield 170 g drained yoghurt. Combine the drained yoghurt with the margarine, flour and salt, and quickly knead to a dough. Wrap the pastry in cling film and refrigerate for at least 2 hours.

2. In the meantime, make the béchamel sauce according to the recipe. Mix in the garlic, grated cheese and basil and season with salt and pepper. Cut the courgettes into 3–4-mm-thick slices.

3. Preheat the oven to 200°C/400°F/gas 6.

4. Roll out the pastry on a floured pastry board. Place the ramekins (about 12 cm in diameter) upside down on the pastry and cut out discs of the same diameter with a sharp knife. Press the dough into the ramekins, pulling it a little up the sides. Cut out 4-cm-wide strips of pastry and line the sides of the ramekins. Prick the base several times with a fork.

1 tsp salt
Pepper
500 g courgettes

5. Fill each ramekin in the following order: 1 layer of courgette slices, 1 thin layer of béchamel sauce, a sprinkling of pepper, another layer of courgette slices, topped with béchamel sauce and another sprinkling of pepper.

6. Bake on the middle shelf for 15–20 minutes, until the quiches turn golden brown.

Tip: A tomato salad makes an excellent accompaniment.

COFFEE CRÊPE WITH ALMONDS

Crêpes au Café aux Amandes

TIME REQUIRED:
45 minutes

1 large or 4 small ovenproof dishes

For the crêpes:
600 ml soya milk
200 g plain flour
2 tbsp chickpea flour
1 pinch salt
Oil, for cooking

For the cream:
500 g soya milk
1 sachet (40 g) vanilla pudding powder
1 tbsp instant coffee
2 tbsp sugar
4 tbsp flaked almonds

Margarine, for greasing

EVERY FRENCH TOWN, no matter how small, has at least one crêperie.

1. For the cream, pour about 120 ml of soya milk into a cup. Add the pudding powder and instant coffee and stir well until free of lumps.

2. Heat the rest of the milk and briskly whisk in the coffee and pudding mixture. Simmer for 1–2 minutes, stirring vigorously, until the cream thickens. Stir in the sugar well and transfer to a bowl. Leave to cool. Set aside in the refrigerator, stirring often.

3. For the crêpes, mix the soya milk with the salt and flours to a smooth batter. Rest for about 15 minutes.

4. Heat 1 tablespoon of oil in a medium, non-stick, shallow frying pan (or crêpe pan). When very hot, pour a ladle of batter into the centre. Gently tilt the pan to spread the batter evenly. Cook for 2–3 minutes and then carefully loosen and lift up the edges of the crêpe with a spatula or palette knife. If the underside is a nice golden colour, flip the crêpe. When the crêpe is a nice golden brown all over, slide it onto a plate and keep warm in the oven. Wipe the pan with kitchen paper and repeat the process until all the batter is used up.

5. Put 2 tablespoons of the cream into the middle of each crêpe and fold over the sides. Put them into the large or four small ovenproof dishes greased with margarine. Sprinkle with flaked almonds. Bake in the oven preheated to 200°C/400°F/gas 6 for 10–15 minutes.

CHEESE CRÊPES WITH WALNUTS AND SHALLOTS BRAISED IN RED WINE

Crêpes au Fromage et aux Noix avec Échalotes au Vin Rouge

TIME REQUIRED: *1 hour*

For the crêpes:
600 ml rice milk
200 g plain flour
2 tbsp chickpea flour
1 pinch salt
Oil, for cooking

For the cream:
Fromage frais (see recipe on page 28)
2 tbsp soya yoghurt
1–2 tsp salt
100 g walnuts, chopped

For the shallots braised in red wine:
4 ramekins or small ovenproof dishes
4 tbsp olive oil
400 g shallots
1 tsp dried thyme
2 tbsp maple syrup or demerara sugar

WHILE SWEET CRÊPES are preferred in Brittany, crêpes are often given savoury fillings in other regions of France. Shallots are particularly popular in the area around Angers, in the Loire Valley. After the harvest, they are stored in well-ventilated sheds and sold all over the world.

1. For the crêpes, mix the ingredients together to a thin crêpe batter.

2. Heat 1 tablespoon of oil in a crêpe pan or non-stick frying pan. Pour a ladle of batter into the centre and gently tilt to spread the batter thinly and evenly. Cook briefly. Loosen the edges with a spatula or palette knife and carefully slide it under the crêpe, then quickly flip the crêpe. Cook the other side briefly and then slide the crêpe onto a plate. Keep warm. Wipe the pan with kitchen paper and repeat the process until all the batter is used up.

3. Heat the olive oil in a frying pan. Peel the shallots, halving the larger ones, and spread them out in the pan. Sauté the shallots until golden brown all over. Turn down the heat, cover the pan tightly with a lid and cook for 4–5 more minutes.

4. Season with the thyme, salt and pepper, and brown, uncovered, for 3 more minutes. Pour the maple syrup over the shallots, or sprinkle with sugar, and take care not to burn the caramel that forms. Deglaze with the red wine and bring to the boil briefly, stirring carefully to dissolve the caramel completely.

5. Preheat the oven to 200°C/400°F/gas 6. Grease the ramekins with oil and distribute the shallots and syrup evenly into them. Put them on a baking tray and braise for about 20 minutes.

125 ml red wine
Salt, pepper
Oil, for greasing

6. For the cream filling, make the fromage frais according to the recipe. Then mix with the yoghurt, salt and chopped walnuts.

7. Fill the crêpes and serve with the braised shallots.

PUMPKIN OMELETTE WITH CREAM SAUCE

Omelette de Potiron à la Crème

TIME REQUIRED: *1 hour*

For the omelette:
1 small pumpkin or red Kuri squash (about 45 g puréed)
2 tbsp olive oil
150 g onions
4 cloves garlic
210 g plain flour
300 ml soya milk
1 tbsp cornflour
½ tsp baking powder
1 tsp paprika
Salt, pepper
Oil, for frying

For the sauce:
200 g fromage frais (see recipe on page 28)
1 tbsp pumpkin seed oil
Salt, pepper
Pumpkin seeds (optional)

Garlic is known as the 'truffle of Provence'. Here, garlic is used to enhance the otherwise bland pumpkin and give the dish its flavour. If you want to spice it up, you can add finely chopped ginger and leek slices to the batter.

1. Preheat the oven to 200°C/400°F/gas 6.
2. Halve, de-seed and coarsely dice the squash. Line a baking sheet with baking parchment. Spread the squash over the tray. Drizzle with the olive oil. Roast the squash until soft, then purée in a bowl with a hand-held blender.
3. Peel and finely chop the onions and garlic. Whisk the soya milk with the flour, cornflour and baking powder in a bowl and incorporate the paprika, onion, garlic and puréed squash. Season well with salt and pepper. Divide the batter into 4 portions.
4. Heat 1 tablespoon of oil in a small non-stick frying pan. Add a portion of the batter, lower the heat and gently fry. When the underside is lightly browned, flip the omelette and cook on the other side until crispy. Keep warm in the oven until the other portions are made.
5. For the sauce, make the fromage frais according to the recipe. Mix with the pumpkin seed oil and, optionally, pumpkin seeds, and season with salt and pepper. Serve with the omelette.

Tip: The omelette can be flipped using a flat plate. Lay the plate over the frying pan and, holding pan and plate in place with a cloth, carefully turn them over at the same time. Then slide the omelette back into the frying pan.

CARROT, CELERIAC AND PEAR TARTE TATIN

Tarte Tatin aux Carottes, Céleri et Poires

TIME REQUIRED:
45 minutes

1 packet vegan puff pastry
300 g celeriac
120 g leeks
250 g carrots
300 g pears
2 tbsp lemon juice
1 tbsp vegan margarine or oil
1 tbsp maple syrup or sugar
1 tsp fennel seeds
Salt

Celeriac contains a great deal of essential oils. The smaller it is cut, the more intense its characteristic flavour becomes.

1. Preheat the oven to 200°C/400°F/gas 6.
2. Wash the celeriac, carrots, leeks and pears. Cut the celeriac and carrots into julienne strips and thinly slice the leeks. Quarter, core and cut the pears into thin wedges. Drizzle everything with the lemon juice.
3. Heat the margarine or oil in a baking dish. For best results, use an oven-safe frying pan with a heat-resistant handle. Gently sauté the fruit and vegetables (over a low heat). Then pour over the maple syrup or sprinkle with sugar and leave to lightly caramelise. Season lightly with salt.
4. Roll out the puff pastry into a disc slightly larger than the diameter of the dish or pan and cover the caramelised fruit and vegetables. Use your fingertips to firmly tuck the pastry around the sides. Bake for 15–20 minutes, until the tart is nicely coloured. Leave to cool a little. Then place a large, flat plate over the dish or pan and turn them over together.

QUICHE PROVENÇALE

TIME REQUIRED:
45 minutes

4 ramekins or small ovenproof dishes, 12–15 cm diameter

1 packet vegan puff pastry
80 g almonds
1 tbsp chopped rosemary
1 tbsp oregano leaves
2 tbsp olive oil
1 shallot
2 cloves garlic
100 g aubergines
100 g courgettes
100 g tomatoes
50 g olives
150 g haricot beans
2 tsp carob powder
1 tbsp lemon juice
4 tbsp coarse dry breadcrumbs
8 cherry tomatoes
Salt, pepper

1. Preheat the oven to 200°C/400°F/gas 6. Line the ramekins with the puff pastry. Press the pastry firmly against the bottom and sides. Prick the base several times with a fork. Cover with aluminium foil and bake for about 15 minutes.

2. Blanch the almonds for 2–3 minutes in boiling water, rinse in cold water and peel off the skin with your fingers. Combine the almonds with the rosemary and oregano and grind to crumbs with a hand-held blender.

3. Peel the shallot and garlic, dice the remaining vegetables and sauté all together in the olive oil. Turn down the heat and cook for 10 minutes.

4. Empty the beans into a sieve, rinse with water and drain. Combine with the cooked vegetables and almond crumbs in a blending beaker and blend briefly. Incorporate the carob flour and season with the lemon juice, salt and pepper.

5. Fill the ramekins with the prebaked pastry with the purée and smooth with a spoon. Cover each ramekin with a tablespoon of breadcrumbs. Slice the cherry tomatoes, arrange them over the quiches and bake for about 20 minutes. Sprinkle the ready-made quiches with freshly ground pepper.

Tip: Make your own breadcrumbs: remove the crust from 1 or 2-day-old sandwich bread and coarsely grind in a food processor, then leave to dry out on a cloth or spread over a baking tray and dry out in the oven, preheated to 160°C/325°F/gas 3, for about 15 minutes. For finer breadcrumbs, simply grind the bread for longer.

MAIN COURSES

CRÊPES WITH GANACHE AND CARAMELISED MELON

Crêpes à la Ganache et Melons Caramélisés

TIME REQUIRED:
45 minutes

For the crêpes:
600 ml almond milk
2 tbsp apple purée
1 pinch salt
200 g plain flour
2 tbsp cornflour
Oil, for cooking

For the ganache:
100 ml vegan cream
100 g dark chocolate
   (70% cocoa)

1 cantaloupe melon
3 tbsp brown sugar or
   maple syrup
50 ml cognac

Crêpes almost always come with a sweet filling in Brittany, such as sugar, jam, fresh fruits and chocolate spread.

1. For the crêpes, combine the almond milk, apple purée, salt, flour and cornflour, and mix well. Rest the batter for 10–15 minutes.
2. Peel, cut up and de-seed the melon. Cut it into 5-mm-thick wedges.
3. For the ganache, coarsely chop the chocolate, heat the vegan cream. Melt the chocolate in the cream. Mix thoroughly and set aside (not in the refrigerator).
4. Heat a tablespoon of oil in a medium non-stick frying pan and pour a ladle of batter into the centre. Gently tilt the pan to spread the batter evenly. Cook for 2–3 minutes and then loosen and lift up the edges of the crêpe with a spatula or palette knife. If the underside is golden brown, flip the crêpe and continue to cook until the edges turn golden brown and crispy. Slide it onto a plate and keep warm in the oven. The finished crêpes can be stacked on top of each other.
5. Melt the sugar in a heavy frying pan. Add the melon wedges and turn them in the caramel. Turn down the heat a little because the caramel will turn bitter if allowed to burn. Pour cognac over everything, if there are no children eating. Gently move the pan back and forth to bind the cognac with the melon pieces.
6. Fill the crêpes with ganache and serve with the caramelised melon.

Tip: Instead of the melon, you can also use apples.

MAIN COURSES

DESSERTS

Chocolate mousse   page 118
Orange and champagne sorbet   page 120
Berry and vanilla cream tart   page 122
Crème caramel   page 124
Nougat and apricot pralines   page 126
Almond biscuits   page 128
Petits fours   page 130
Chocolate and strawberry cream tartlets   page 132
Hazelnut and fig clafoutis   page 134
Pear crumble   page 136
Tarte tatin   page 138
Grape and yoghurt cream tart   page 140
Armagnac cake   page 142
Madeleines   page 144
Macarons   page 146
Strawberry tart   page 148
Rum truffles   page 150
Raspberry parfait   page 152
Chocolate cake   page 154
Raspberry liqueur   page 156
Vin d'orange   page 158
French toast with raspberry sauce   page 160
Apple and champagne tart   page 162

CHOCOLATE MOUSSE

Mousse au Chocolat

TIME REQUIRED:
15 minutes + 3 hours refrigeration time

200 g silken tofu
1 tbsp sugar
½ tsp Bourbon vanilla powder
150 g dark chocolate (70% cocoa)
250 g vegan whipped spray cream (or soya cream whipped with whipped cream stabiliser)
Some sprigs of peppermint

Chocolate mousse is a luscious treat with a fluffy and light consistency.

1. Squeeze the tofu and mix with the sugar and vanilla.
2. Melt the chocolate over a bain-marie, leave to cool and mix with the tofu.
3. Gently fold in the whipped cream and refrigerate for 3 hours.
4. Garnish with peppermint and serve.

ORANGE AND CHAMPAGNE SORBET

Sorbet à l'Orange

TIME REQUIRED:
15 minutes + 8 hours refrigeration time

6 (about 300 g) oranges, squeezed
3 tsp Cointreau
200 ml champagne
50 ml water
100 g sugar

Sorbet is a semi-frozen dessert made from puréed fruit, fruit juice and sugar. Alcohol can also be added. Sorbet has a special smooth consistency that requires stirring several times as it freezes.

1. Bring the water to the boil with the sugar. Turn down the heat and simmer for 3 minutes. Stir in the orange juice, Cointreau and champagne.
2. Strain the mixture through a fine-mesh sieve into a shallow container and place in the freezer. After 2 hours, stir the mixture with a fork, then repeat the process every hour.
3. Freeze for a total of 8 hours. During this time, whisk the sorbet with a hand-held blender (in a blending beaker). Whisk it again before serving for a soft and smooth consistency.

Tip: A sparkling wine such as prosecco can be used instead of champagne.

BERRY AND VANILLA CREAM TART
Tarte aux Fruits Rouges et Crème Vanille

TIME REQUIRED: *80 minutes + 1–2 hours refrigeration time*

Tart mould (28 cm in diameter)

For the shortcrust pastry:
300 g wholemeal flour
2 tsp baking powder
100 g muscovado sugar, finely ground
200 g high-quality vegan margarine
About 4 tbsp water
Vegan margarine, for greasing

For the vanilla cream:
250 ml rice milk
1 packet vanilla pudding powder
Sugar (as needed)
2 heaped tbsp soya cream, whipped

1. Mix the flour with the baking powder and sift the mixture onto a pastry board. Make a well in the centre. Put the sugar into the well and spread the margarine in small pieces over the flour. Add the water and quickly knead to a smooth dough. Roll the pastry into a ball, cover with aluminium foil and rest in the refrigerator for 1–2 hours.

2. In the meantime, make the vanilla cream. Bring the rice milk to the boil in a pan. Before it comes to the boil, mix 5 tablespoons of the warm milk with the pudding powder until no lumps remain. Whisk the mixture into the boiling milk, then simmer for 2–3 minutes, stirring constantly, until the pudding mixture thickens. Transfer to a bowl, stir in sugar as needed and leave to cool. Stir often. Fold in the whipped cream shortly before assembling the tart.

3. Preheat the oven to 200°C/400°F/gas 6. Grease the tart mould. Roll out the pastry on a floured pastry board to a 1–1½-cm-thick sheet and line the bottom and sides of the mould. Prick the bottom all over with a fork at closely spaced intervals. With the oven shelf on the second position from the bottom, bake for

For the topping:
1 handful fresh raspberries
1 handful fresh blueberries
10 large fresh strawberries
10 lemon balm leaves (optional)
1 sachet vegan glaze (optional)

about 25 minutes, until golden brown. Leave the tart case to cool a little and then turn it out onto a rack.

4. Wash and sort the berries.

5. Spread the vanilla cream over the bottom of the tart case, then top with the berries and garnish with lemon balm leaves. Prepare the glaze according to the instructions on the packet and spread sparingly over the tart.

CRÈME CARAMEL

TIME REQUIRED:
30 minutes

Ramekins or small ovenproof dishes

For the cream:
800 ml rice milk
400 ml oat cream
4 tbsp durum wheat semolina
1 packet vanilla sugar
4 tbsp plain flour

For the caramel:
100 g sugar or muscovado sugar
120 ml water
120 ml oat cream

CRÈME CARAMEL is a custard dessert that is usually made by cooking eggs, milk and sugar over a bain-marie. Caramel, which is poured over the top before serving, actually means 'burnt sugar'.

1. Preheat the oven to 180°C/350°F/gas 4.
2. Combine the rice milk and cream in a pan and bring to the boil. Use a wooden spoon to slowly stir in the semolina and vanilla sugar. Keep stirring as the mixture tends to stick to the bottom of the pan. Incorporate the flour, turn down the heat and simmer, stirring constantly, until the cream bubbles and thickens. Fill the ramekins, leave to cool and refrigerate for 2 hours.
3. For the caramel, combine the sugar and water in a small saucepan and place over a low heat until the sugar dissolves. Simmer the syrup for about 5 minutes, stirring constantly, until a dark caramel forms. Stir in the oat cream until smooth.
4. Turn out the contents of the ramekins and pour the warm caramel sauce over the top.

Tip: You can also sprinkle a tablespoon of muscovado sugar over the ramekins and caramelise it with a kitchen blow torch to form a crunchy crust.

NOUGAT AND APRICOT PRALINES

Pralines au Nougat et aux Abricots

TIME REQUIRED: *1 hour + refrigeration time*

Makes about 25

25 foil cake cases

10 dried apricots
3 tbsp cognac
125 g dark couverture chocolate (80% cocoa)
60 g almond nougat
20 g white rice milk chocolate
4 tsp oat cream

The German cook to the French aristocrat, Comte de Plessis-Praslin, is believed to have invented the praline in the seventeenth century.

1. Quarter seven dried apricots and soak overnight in 2 tablespoons of cognac.

2. Melt the couverture chocolate over a bain-marie. Put a teaspoon of the chocolate into each foil case and line them by tilting from side to side (the chocolate shouldn't be too warm). Place the foil cases upside down on a rack to cool.

3. Combine the nougat and white chocolate, melt over a bain-marie and incorporate the oat cream. Stir in a tablespoon of cognac.

4. Put a soaked apricot quarter into each of the prepared moulds, fill with the nougat cream and refrigerate for about 1 hour. Melt the remaining couverture chocolate again over a bain-marie and fill the moulds to the brim.

5. Cut the remaining three dried apricots into thin strips and decorate the top of each praline with three strips before the chocolate hardens.

6. Store in an airtight jar in the refrigerator.

Tip: You can also use this recipe to make marzipan and apricot pralines by simply substituting the nougat cream (for this, combine 80 g marzipan with 20 g sifted icing sugar and 1 tablespoon cognac and knead well).

Desserts

ALMOND BISCUITS

Biscuits aux Amandes

TIME REQUIRED:
20 minutes

Makes 12

70 g silken tofu
1–3 tbsp oil
1 tbsp plant-based milk
1 tsp almond liqueur or almond essence
70 g plain flour
½ tsp baking powder
50 g sugar
1 pinch Bourbon vanilla powder
70 g flaked almonds
1 pinch salt
12 almonds
100 g vegan dark couverture chocolate

Almonds thrive particularly well in Provence. This type of almond biscuit is also called a macaroon not to be confused with a French macaron, which is very different.

1. Squeeze the tofu well (leaving about 45 g) and mix it with the oil, plant-based milk and almond liqueur.
2. Sift the flour with the baking powder and then mix with the sugar and vanilla. Mix the wet and dry ingredients together and use a wooden spoon to stir in the almond flakes.
3. Preheat the oven to 180°C/350°F/gas 4. Use two teaspoons to form balls with the dough and place them on a baking tray lined with baking parchment. Insert an almond into the middle of each. Bake on the middle shelf for 15–20 minutes.
4. Melt the chocolate over a bain-marie and dip the bottom third of each biscuit in the chocolate. Leave to dry on a sheet of aluminium foil.

PETITS FOURS

TIME REQUIRED:
40 minutes

Makes 12

For the cakes:
350 g plain flour
1 tbsp baking powder
150 g sugar
1 sachet vanilla sugar
250 g soya yoghurt
50 ml soda water
120 ml oil
4 tbsp raspberry or blueberry jam
200 g marzipan
80 g icing sugar

For the icing:
250 g fondant icing, for melting
Raspberry or blueberry syrup (optional)

Petits fours are small and delicate French cakes and pastries. They received their name ('petit four' literally means 'small oven'), because they were originally baked in the residual heat of the oven after the main items were cooked at high heat (known as 'grand four' or 'big oven').

1. Sift the flour with the baking powder. Mix the sugar with the vanilla sugar and soya yoghurt. Mix in the flour and incorporate the soda water and oil.

2. Preheat the oven to 180°C/350°F/gas 4. Line a baking tray with baking parchment and spread the batter evenly inside. Bake on the middle shelf for 25–30 minutes, until light golden. Leave to cool.

3. Halve the sponge sheet, cut each half into a 16 x 12-cm rectangle and spread with jam. Lay one over the other with the jam facing upwards.

4. Mix the marzipan with the icing sugar and roll it out on a work surface dusted with icing sugar. Lay the sheet over the jam. Cut the cake into twelve 4-cm squares by cutting twice lengthways and three times across its width.

5. Melt the fondant over a bain-marie heated to 36–40°C and mix with the syrup and lemon juice. Use a teaspoon to quickly spread the mixture over the cake squares.

Juice of ½ lemon
Icing sugar, for dusting the work surface

Tip: You can also ice the petits fours with a lemon glacé icing. You need 500 g icing sugar, 80 ml water, the juice of half a lemon and a little raspberry syrup to colour the glaze pink. Sift the icing sugar into a bowl and mix well with the lemon juice, raspberry syrup and water to a spreadable paste.

CHOCOLATE AND STRAWBERRY CREAM TARTLETS

Tartelettes au Chocolat à la Crème de Fraise

TIME REQUIRED:
30 minutes + refrigeration and baking time

Makes 6 small tartlets (5 cm in diameter) or 4 large tartlets (8 cm in diameter)

For the tartlets:
150 g plain flour
1 pinch baking powder
25 g cocoa powder
40 g caster sugar
80 g high-quality vegan margarine, softened

For the cream:
200 g strawberries (6 for decoration)
2 tbsp icing sugar
1½ tsp arrowroot
200 g soya cream
1 sachet whipped cream stabiliser
Vegan dark couverture chocolate, melted
Icing sugar, for dusting
Dried beans or rice, for blind baking

Patîsseries in France typically offer tartlets with a lemon or chocolate filling, but variations with different fruits are quite popular.

1. Sift the flour with the baking powder and quickly knead with the cocoa, sugar and margarine into a dough. Wrap the pastry in cling film or aluminium foil and refrigerate for 1 hour.
2. Grease tartlet moulds by brushing with plenty of margarine and dusting with flour. Preheat the oven to 200°C/400°F/gas 6.
3. Line the bottom and sides of the moulds with the pastry. Cover the insides with baking parchment and fill with the beans or rice. Bake on the middle shelf for 15 minutes. Then remove the paper and weights and bake for 10 more minutes. Turn the tart cases out of the moulds and leave to cool on a rack.
4. For the cream, purée the strawberries with a hand-held blender. Combine with the icing sugar in a saucepan and bring to the boil while stirring constantly. Dissolve the arrowroot in 20 ml of water and whisk it into the strawberry purée. Cook for 2 minutes. Whip the soya cream with the stabiliser and fold into the strawberry purée. Refrigerate for 2–3 hours.
5. For the decoration, halve the whole strawberries and dip them in the melted chocolate.
6. Transfer the strawberry cream to a piping bag fitted with a large nozzle and pipe swirls into the tartlet cases. Decorate with the chocolate-coated strawberries and dust with icing sugar.

Tip: If stored in a dry place, the cases will keep like shortbread biscuits. You can prepare them beforehand and fill them at a later time.

HAZELNUT AND FIG CLAFOUTIS

Clafoutis aux Figues et Noisettes

TIME REQUIRED:
35 minutes

4 ramekins or small ovenproof dishes

6 chestnuts, roasted and peeled
70 g high-quality vegan margarine
50 g sugar
1 sachet vanilla sugar
½ tsp ground cinnamon
50 hazelnuts
100 ml plant-based milk
1 tbsp apple purée
100 g plain flour
3 figs
1 tbsp vegan margarine, for greasing

Clafoutis is a soft pudding that originated in the Limousin region. This popular dessert is traditionally made with cherries, although figs, peaches or apricots can also be used.

1. Preheat the oven to 200°C/400°F/gas 6. Grease 4 ramekins with one tablespoon of margarine.
2. Slice the chestnuts. Mix the margarine until fluffy and add the sugar, vanilla, cinnamon and hazelnuts. Mix in the plant-based milk and apple purée, and fold in the flour and chestnuts. Divide the batter into the ramekins.
3. Wash, dry and quarter the figs and arrange them over the batter.
4. Bake in the middle of the oven for 25–30 minutes. Leave to cool a little and serve.

Desserts

PEAR CRUMBLE

Crumble aux Poires

TIME REQUIRED:
10 minutes + 20 minutes baking time

4 glass ramekins (6 cm in diameter and 7 cm deep)

400 g sour pears
Juice of 1 lemon
25 cranberries or barberries
10 walnut halves
40 g sugar
50 g high-quality vegan margarine, cold
70 g wheat or spelt flour
1 tsp grated lemon zest
Sugar, for sprinkling

Many pear varieties with famous names originated in France. King Louis XIV is said to have particularly loved the Louise Bonne pear.

1. Wash, core and cut the pears into wedges or pieces and drizzle with the lemon juice. Layer with the berries and walnuts in the ramekins.

2. Preheat the oven to 180°C/350°F/gas 4.

3. Quickly knead together the sugar with the margarine, flour and lemon zest and roughly cover the pears with the mixture. Sprinkle over with a little sugar and bake on the middle shelf for 20–25 minutes.

Tip: For this dessert, it is best to use firm, sour fruit (apples, plums, apricots, rhubarb).

TARTE TATIN

TIME REQUIRED: *1 hour + 1 hour resting time*

Oven-safe frying pan (about 26 cm in diameter)

For the pastry:
250 g plain flour (or spelt flour, optionally)
1 tsp baking powder
2 tbsp apple purée
120 g high-quality vegan margarine, softened
1 tbsp icing sugar
1 sachet vanilla sugar
1 pinch salt

For the filling:
1 kg sour apples
150 g icing sugar
2 tbsp apple juice
100 g high-quality vegan margarine

TARTE TATIN is also known in Paris as 'tarte du chef' or 'tarte des demoiselles Tatin'. The characteristic caramel layer is created by baking it upside down, before turning it over.

1. Prepare an oven-safe frying pan with a heavy bottom, preferably in stainless steel.
2. Sift the flour with the baking powder into a bowl. Add the apple purée, margarine, sugar, vanilla sugar and salt, and mix together. Gently knead the pastry. Wrap the pastry in cling film and refrigerate for at least 1 hour.
3. In the meantime, peel, core and quarter the apples (cut smaller apples into eighths).
4. Make a 1-cm-deep layer with 120 g of icing sugar in the frying pan and drizzle with the apple juice. Arrange the apple pieces in a layer over the sugar. Melt 80 g of margarine and pour over the apples. Place the pan over a low heat. Turn the apples over continuously in the resulting caramel. When the apples are half-soft, heat the remaining margarine and drizzle over them and sprinkle with the rest of the icing sugar.
5. Preheat the oven to 200°C/400°F/gas 6. Roll out the pastry on a floured work surface into a disc the same diameter as that of the pan. Carefully cover the apples with the pastry, pressing lightly around the edges. Bake in the middle of the oven for 25–30 minutes, until the pastry turns golden brown.
6. Take the pan out of the oven, cover with a plate and turn the tart over. It is delicious hot or cold.

Tip: This tasty tart can also be made with plums, apricots or pears.

GRAPE AND YOGHURT CREAM TART

Tarte à la Crème et aux Raisins

TIME REQUIRED:
40 minutes

Tart mould (18 cm in diameter)

500 g soya yoghurt
2 tbsp icing sugar
1 sachet vanilla sugar
500 g grapes
1 packet vegan spelt puff pastry
Icing sugar, for dusting
Dried beans, lentils or rice, for blind baking

Tarts need not always be made using the typical shortcrust pastry. Puff pastry is a very good, quick and particularly uncomplicated alternative.

1. Drain the yoghurt overnight in a sieve lined with a cotton cloth (you can also use a coffee filter to line the sieve). Put the drained yoghurt into a bowl and mix with the icing and vanilla sugar. Set aside in the refrigerator. Wash the grapes.

2. Preheat the oven to 200°C/400°F/gas 6. Roll out the puff pastry and line a tart mould (18 cm in diameter). Press down well. Lightly fold over any excess dough. Cover the pastry with baking parchment and fill to a 1-cm depth with dried beans. Bake for 10 minutes, until the pastry turns golden. Turn the pastry out of the mould and remove the beans and parchment. Prick the base of the tart case all over with a fork and return it to the oven. Bake until it turns a crispy golden brown.

3. Leave the tart case to cool, then fill it with the yoghurt cream and top with grapes. Finally, dust the tart with icing sugar.

ARMAGNAC CAKE

Gâteau à l'Armagnac

TIME REQUIRED:
15 minutes + baking time

Loaf tin (30 x 11 cm)

100 g high-quality vegan margarine
100 g golden caster sugar
1 tsp grated lemon zest
2 tbsp apple purée
125 ml soya milk
125 ml soda water
250 g plain flour
1 sachet vanilla pudding powder
1 tbsp baking powder
50 g icing sugar
50 ml armagnac
Oil and flour, for greasing

Armagnac is a brandy distilled from the white wine produced in the Gascony region. It has a more fiery flavour than cognac and is typically served after meals.

1. Grease a loaf tin (30 x 11 cm) with margarine and dust with flour. Preheat the oven to 200°C/400°F/gas 6.

2. Mix the margarine with the caster sugar, lemon zest and apple purée until fluffy. Mix the soya milk with the soda water. Sift the flour with the pudding powder and baking powder and fold a little at a time, alternating with the milk and water mixture, into the margarine and sugar mixture. Pour the batter into the loaf tin. Bake on the bottom shelf for 50–60 minutes (check it is cooked by inserting a wooden chopstick into the cake – if it comes out clean, the cake is done). If the surface of the cake starts to turn too dark, cover it with aluminium foil.

3. Leave the cake to cool a little and turn it out of the tin. Mix the icing sugar with the armagnac and sprinkle the mixture over the cake.

MADELEINES

TIME REQUIRED:
30 minutes + baking time

Madeleine mould to make 12

50 g rice (or rice flour)
50 g semolina (durum wheat) flour
5 g cream of tartar
1 pinch salt
50 g almonds
60 ml rapeseed oil
30 ml almond cooking cream
50 g muscovado sugar, finely ground
1 tbsp vanilla powder
½ tsp grated orange zest

THE SHAPE OF madeleines is reminiscent of the relief of a scallop shell. These fine pastries originated in Commercy and are believed to have been named after a cook.

1. Preheat the oven to 180°C/350°F/gas 4. Grease the madeleine mould with oil and dust with flour.

2. Finely grind the rice and sift with the semolina flour, cream of tartar and salt. Blanch the almonds in boiling water, drain in a sieve, refresh in cold water and peel. Briefly dry them out in the oven and grind. Whisk the oil with the almond cream. Incorporate the sugar, vanilla and orange zest, followed by the ground almonds.

3. Quickly knead the ingredients together to a dough and press cleanly into the mould cavities, making sure there is no excess.

4. Bake on the middle shelf for 8–10 minutes. Leave the madeleines to cool and then turn them out of the mould.

Desserts

MACARONS

TIME REQUIRED:
30 minutes + 3 hours 30 minutes baking time

Makes about 30

Piping bag with plain nozzle (8 mm in diameter)
Baking parchment or baking mats for macarons

120 g aquafaba (liquid from about 1 tin chickpeas)
80 g almonds, blanched and finely ground
70 g icing sugar
1 tsp lemon juice
60 g sugar
Green food colouring (powder)

For the cream:
110 g non-hydrogenated plant-based margarine, softened

1. Drain the chickpeas in a sieve over a bowl and collect the aquafaba. Weigh it out to obtain the exact weight required. Put it into a pan, bring to the boil and reduce by half (10 minutes). Weigh it out to obtain the exact amount required, you will need 60 g. Leave to cool.

2. Mix the ground almonds with the icing sugar in a bowl.

3. Combine the aquafaba and lemon juice and beat with a hand mixer or a food processor at high speed until frothy (3–4 minutes). Then add the sugar a little at a time. Continue to beat on the highest speed setting to stiff peaks. Add the food colouring and beat until the batter is uniformly coloured (you can make the colour very bright because it will fade noticeably when baked).

4. Fold the green mixture into the almond mixture. Then work the batter by spreading it over the bottom of the bowl until it turns viscous.

5. Line two baking trays with baking parchment or baking mats. Transfer the batter to a piping bag and pipe discs as uniformly as possible (about 3.5 cm in diameter).

6. The trick now is to remove the bubbles from the batter and make the surface smooth. To do this, simply tap the tray firmly from below with the ball of your thumb.

7. Leave the macaron shells to dry for about 2 hours.

8. Preheat the oven to 110°C/225°F/gas ¼. Then bake the macarons with the oven shelf on the second position from the top for 30 minutes. It's important to keep the oven door closed. Turn off the oven and leave the macaron shells inside without opening the door for 30 more minutes.

120 g vegan fromage frais (see recipe on page 28)
100 g icing sugar
1 vanilla pod
1 tbsp finely grated lemon zest (organic)
Or
1 tbsp finely grated orange zest (organic)

9. In the meantime, make the cream. Split the vanilla pod and scrape out the seeds with a knife. Beat the margarine with the fromage frais with a hand mixer until creamy and then gradually incorporate the icing sugar, vanilla seeds and lemon or orange zest. Cover and set aside in the refrigerator until ready to use.

10. Take the macaron shells out of the oven and cool completely on a rack.

11. Sort the shells into pairs by size for filling. Pipe a small amount of the filling onto an upturned shell and cover it with the other.

12. The macarons can be stored in an airtight container for 12–24 hours in the refrigerator.

STRAWBERRY TART

Tarte aux Fraises

TIME REQUIRED:
25 minutes + baking time

Springform cake tin or tart mould (28 cm in diameter)

For the tart case:
200 g finely ground wholemeal spelt or wheat flour
1 sachet cream of tartar
1 pinch salt
80 g muscovado sugar, finely ground
1 tbsp vanilla powder
1 tsp grated lemon zest (organic)
8 g ground linseed
60 ml water
45 ml rapeseed oil or another neutral oil
200 ml rice milk

For the nut butter:
100 g chopped hazelnuts
Muscovado sugar (optional)

250 g fresh strawberries
Vegan glaze (optional)

1. Preheat the oven to 180°C/350°F/gas 4. Line a springform tin with baking parchment.

2. Sift the flour with the cream of tartar and salt into a bowl. Mix the sugar with the vanilla and lemon zest.

3. Mix the linseed with the water and hydrate for about 5 minutes, then whisk with the oil and rice milk.

4. Briskly mix together all the ingredients with a spoon. Pour the batter into the springform tin and spread it higher around the sides to prevent the middle from bulging as the tart case is baked.

5. Bake on the middle shelf for 25–30 minutes, then take out and leave to cool. Remove the sides of the tin and peel off the parchment.

6. For the nut butter, grind the hazelnuts with a hand-held blender to a smooth paste. Sweeten with a little muscovado sugar if desired. Spread the nut butter over the tart case and top with a layer of sliced strawberries. Optionally, glaze the top of the tart with the vegan glaze.

RUM TRUFFLES

Truffes au Rhum

TIME REQUIRED:
30 minutes + cooling time

Makes 20–30 truffles

50 g dark chocolate (75% cocoa)
3 tsp rum (38% alcohol)
40 g almonds, blanched and finely ground
20 g walnuts, finely ground
30 g vegan margarine
4 tbsp icing sugar
50 g icing sugar or cocoa powder

1. Melt the chocolate over a bain-marie and mix with the rum.
2. Add the nuts and mix well.
3. Beat the margarine with the sifted icing sugar until fluffy and incorporate one teaspoon at a time into the chocolate mixture.
4. Shape about a teaspoon of the mixture into small balls and put them into a bowl with the icing sugar or cocoa powder. Shake the bowl in a circular motion.
5. Chill the truffles in the refrigerator and then use a sieve to sprinkle with the remaining icing sugar or cocoa powder.
6. Store in an airtight jar in the refrigerator.

RASPBERRY PARFAIT

Parfait aux Framboises

TIME REQUIRED:
20 minutes+ cooling time

350 ml vegan cream
300 ml coconut milk
60 g sugar
1 tbsp cornflour
100 g coconut flour
1 sachet vanilla sugar
50 g raspberries
50 ml aquafaba (chickpea water)
½ tsp cream of tartar

Raspberries, to accompany

Parfait, which means 'perfect', is a dessert that is served semi-frozen. However, unlike ice cream and sorbet, it is frozen in a mould instead of churning or stirring.

1. Combine the vegan cream, coconut milk, sugar, cornflour, coconut flour and vanilla sugar in a pan and bring to the boil while stirring constantly. Remove the pan from the heat and leave to cool.

2. Put the raspberries into a saucepan over a medium heat, bring to the boil and then purée. Leave to cool.

3. Incorporate into the coconut mixture.

4. Drain the chickpeas in a sieve over a bowl and collect the aquafaba. Beat the aquafaba with the cream of tartar with a hand mixer or in a food processor at high speed until frothy, and then to stiff peaks.

5. Quickly fold it into the coconut and raspberry mixture.

6. Line a loaf tin with cling film and fill it with the parfait mixture.

7. Freeze for about 8 hours. Take the parfait out of the freezer and leave to thaw for at least 15 minutes before serving with fresh raspberries.

CHOCOLATE CAKE

Gâteau au Chocolat

TIME REQUIRED:
45 minutes

5–6 small cake moulds (depending on size)

100 g sugar
1 sachet vanilla sugar
1 tbsp cocoa powder
180 g plain flour
1 tbsp cornflour
2 tsp baking powder
1 pinch salt
80 g dark chocolate (70% cocoa)
180 g vegan margarine
1 tbsp apple cider vinegar
100 ml soya milk
Icing sugar, for dusting
Vegan margarine + 1 tbsp flour, for greasing

This small and delicate chocolate cake should be enjoyed while it's still warm.

1. Preheat the oven to 180°C/350°F/gas 4. Slide the shelf into the second position from the bottom. Grease the moulds with margarine and dust the inside with flour.

2. Mix the sugar, vanilla sugar and cocoa powder. Sift together the flour, cornflour, baking powder and salt.

3. Melt the chocolate with the margarine over a bain-marie.

4. Stir the vinegar into the soya milk.

5. First, stir the sugar, vanilla and cocoa mixture into the chocolate and margarine mixture. Then add the coagulated soya milk and sift the flour mixture over the top. Mix everything thoroughly with a fork.

6. Fill the greased moulds a little over halfway and bake for about 25 minutes.

7. Leave to cool a little. Run a sharp knife around the sides of the moulds to loosen the cakes and turn them out onto plates. Dust with icing sugar and serve warm.

Desserts

RASPBERRY LIQUEUR

Liqueur de Framboise

TIME REQUIRED:
20 minutes + ageing time

*500 g raspberries
 (frozen or fresh)
200 g sugar
500 ml cognac
100 g sugar
250 ml water*

Liqueurs are alcoholic beverages made with at least 100 grams of sugar per litre and aromatic ingredients. Cognac is double distilled and aged in old oak barrels.

1. Mix the frozen raspberries with 200 g of sugar and about 2 tablespoons of water in a pan and heat briefly (fresh raspberries should only be mixed with the sugar). Pour in the cognac and transfer the mixture to a glass bottle with an airtight lid.
2. Age for 4 weeks at room temperature, shaking the bottle well every day.
3. Pour the liquid through muslin or a filter into a bowl.
4. Combine 100 g of sugar with 250 ml of water in a pan and bring to the boil. Simmer for 10 minutes and add the syrup to the alcoholic mixture.
5. Filter the liquid again, fill the bottles and seal them with a cork.

VIN D'ORANGE

TIME REQUIRED:
10 minutes + 10 days

500 ml rosé wine
500 ml white wine
3 untreated oranges
1 small cinnamon stick
3 cloves
1 vanilla pod
Rock sugar (or stevia or maple syrup), for sweetening (optional)

VIN D'ORANGE IS a fruity alcoholic speciality from the south of France. When vin d'orange is served as an apéritif, very little sugar should be added to preserve the bitter flavour. However, it should taste sweet if served as a dessert wine.

1. Mix the wines in a glass bowl.
2. Wash the oranges and peel off strips of zest (avoid removing any pith) with a vegetable peeler.
3. Add the zest, cinnamon, cloves and vanilla to the wine mixture. Sweeten if desired.
4. Cover with a cloth and leave to steep for at least 10 days.
5. Filter through a sieve into an attractive bottle and store in the refrigerator.

Desserts

FRENCH TOAST WITH RASPBERRY SAUCE

Pain Perdu sur Miroir Framboise

TIME REQUIRED:
45 minutes

6 slices white bread, thick-sliced for toasting
250 g apple purée
50 g chickpea flour
70 ml soda water
1 sachet vanilla sugar
200 ml rapeseed oil
150 ml vegan cream
1 tbsp whipped cream stabiliser
Icing sugar, for dusting
4 small sprigs peppermint
1 handful mixed fruits
250 g raspberries (fresh or frozen)

This dessert is an excellent option for a Sunday brunch and also makes a good main course for those of us with a sweet tooth if served in a larger portion.

1. Cut the slices of bread diagonally into triangles and toast them lightly (this can also be done in the oven).
2. Mix the apple purée with the chickpea flour, vanilla and soda water to a thick batter.
3. Cover the bottom of a frying pan with rapeseed oil (about 2 tablespoons) and heat. Dip the bread triangles in the batter and fry in the oil until golden brown all over. Drain on kitchen paper.
4. Whip the cream with the stabiliser.
5. Purée the raspberries.
6. Arrange the French toast on a plate and dust with icing sugar and add the raspberry sauce, cream and mixed fruits. Garnish with peppermint.

APPLE AND CHAMPAGNE TART

Gâteau aux Pommes et au Champagne

TIME REQUIRED:
1 hour + baking time + refrigeration time

Tart mould (24 cm in diameter)

For the pastry:
250 g plain flour
130 g vegan margarine, cold
70 g sugar
3 tbsp white wine
Vegan margarine and flour, for greasing

For the filling:
1 kg apples
500 ml apple juice
500 ml champagne
180 g sugar
1 sachet vanilla sugar
2 sachets vanilla pudding powder
250 ml vegan cream, whipped
1 sachet whipped cream stabiliser

Only sparkling wine made in the Champagne wine region with grapes that are grown and pressed under strictly controlled conditions are allowed to be called champagne.

1. Use a knife to cut pieces of the cold margarine into the flour and rub them in with your fingers until crumbs form.
2. Knead in the remaining pastry ingredients together to a dough, then wrap the pastry in cling film or aluminium foil and rest in the refrigerator for 30 minutes.
3. Preheat the oven to 180°C/350°F/gas 4.
4. Grease the tart mould with margarine and dust with flour. Roll out the pastry on a floured work surface. Cut out a disc large enough to cover the bottom and sides of the mould, then line the mould.
5. Peel, core and cut the apples into wedges. Fill the mould to the top with the apple wedges.
6. Combine the apple juice, champagne, sugar and vanilla sugar in a pan, setting aside a quarter of the cold liquid, and bring to the boil. Dissolve the pudding powder with the cold liquid and then whisk the mixture into the boiling liquid. Cook until the pudding mixture thickens, stirring constantly.
7. Pour the hot pudding mixture over the apples.
8. Bake the tart on the bottom shelf for 90 minutes. Leave the tart to cool and then refrigerate for at least 12 hours to become firm.
9. Beat the vegan cream with the stabiliser. Transfer the tart from the mould to a plate. The centre of the tart will have sunken slightly. Cover the tart with a mound of whipped cream.

Tip: You can easily use a light, diluted fruit juice instead of the champagne or sparkling wine. Diluted elderflower cordial is a good alternative.

INDEX

A
Aïoli 20
Almonds
    Almond biscuits 128
    Coffee crêpe with almonds 104
    Herbes de Provence and almond terrine with beetroot salad 44
    Madeleines 144
    Quiche provençale 112
    Stuffed spinach with potato and almond balls 92
Apple
    Apple and champagne tart 162
    Bitter salad with apple and juniper vinaigrette 52
    Tarte tatin 138
Apricots
    Apricot croissants 18
    Nougat and apricot pralines 126
Armagnac cake 142
Artichokes
    Artichoke purée with baguette and olive paste 40
    Artichokes with two dips 42
    Stuffed artichokes cooked in red wine 82
Asparagus
    Baked asparagus with herb sauce and duchess potatoes 70
Aubergines
    Aubergine and lemon gratin 86
    Provence-style lentils with cashew cheese 80
    Quiche provençale 112
    Ratatouille with roasted potato slices 94

B
Baguette 14
    Artichoke purée with baguette and olive paste 40
    Baguette and vegetable gratin 78
    Porcini mushrooms with walnuts and cranberry vinaigrette 84
Beans
    Quiche provençale 112
    Red bean and mushroom pie 72
    Sauerkraut tart 64
Béchamel sauce 30
Beetroot
    Herbes de Provence and almond terrine with beetroot salad 44
Berries
    Berry and vanilla cream tart 122
    French toast with raspberry sauce 160
    Raspberry liqueur 156
    Raspberry parfait 152
Brioches 16
Broccoli
    Baguette and vegetable gratin 78

C
Cakes
    Armagnac cake 142
    Chocolate cake 154
    Madeleines 144
    Petits fours 130

Caramel
- Crème Caramel 124
- Tarte tatin 138

Carrots
- Carrot, celeriac and pear tarte tatin 110

Cashews
- Provence-style lentils with cashew cheese 80
- Tomato and cashew cream tart 58

Cauliflower
- Cauliflower soufflé pie 90

Celeriac
- Carrot, celeriac and pear tarte tatin 110
- Chestnut soup 38

Champagne
- Apple and champagne tart 162
- Braised fennel with champagne sauce 96
- Orange and champagne sorbet 120

Chestnuts
- Chestnut soup 38
- Hazelnut and fig clafoutis 134
- Red cabbage stew 98

Chickpeas
- Artichoke purée with baguette and olive paste 40
- Macarons 146
- Spinach, chickpea and hazelnut omelette 66

Chocolate
- Chocolate and strawberry cream tartlets 132
- Chocolate cake 154
- Chocolate mousse 118
- Crêpes with ganache and caramelised melon 114
- Nougat and apricot pralines 126

Clafoutis
- Hazelnut and fig clafoutis 134

Courgettes
- Courgette quiche 102
- Provence-style lentils with cashew cheese 80
- Quiche provençale 112
- Ratatouille with roasted potato slices 94
- Vegetable terrine with marinated spring onions 46

Crêpes
- Cheese crêpes with walnuts and shallots braised in red wine 106
- Coffee crêpe with almonds 104
- Crêpes with Cointreau cream and oranges 100
- Crêpes with ganache and caramelised melon 114

Crumble
- Pear crumble 136

F

Fennel
- Braised fennel with champagne sauce 96
- Carrot, celeriac and pear tarte tatin 110
- Chestnut soup 38
- Pear and fennel salad with caramelised nuts and grapes 48

Figs
- Hazelnut and fig clafoutis 134

Fromage frais 28

G

Grapes
- Grape and yoghurt cream tart 140
- Herbes de Provence and almond terrine with beetroot salad 44
- Mushroom and grape tartlets 68
- Pear and fennel salad with caramelised nuts and grapes 48

Gratin
- Aubergine and lemon gratin 86
- Baguette and vegetable gratin 78
- Gratin dauphinois 88

H
Hazelnuts
- Hazelnut and fig clafoutis 134
- Spinach, chickpea and hazelnut omelette 66
- Strawberry tart 148

Herbes de Provence and almond terrine with beetroot salad 44

L
Leek
- Baguette and vegetable gratin 78
- Carrot, celeriac and pear tarte tatin 110
- Leek soup 50

Lemons
- Aubergine and lemon gratin 86
- Stuffed artichokes cooked in red wine 82

Lentils
- Lentil and pumpkin stew 74
- Provence-style lentils with cashew cheese 80

Liqueur
- Raspberry liqueur 156

M
Macarons 146

Madeleines 144

Melon
- Crêpes with ganache and caramelised melon 114

Mushrooms
- Breaded mushrooms with mustard sauce 76
- Mushroom and grape tartlets 68
- Porcini mushrooms with walnuts and cranberry vinaigrette 84
- Provence-style lentils with cashew cheese 80
- Red bean and mushroom pie 72
- Stuffed spinach with potato and almond balls 92

N
Nougat and apricot pralines 126

O
Olives
- Artichoke purée with baguette and olive paste 40
- Olive paste 24
- Pissaladière – Provençal pizza 60
- Provence-style lentils with cashew cheese 80
- Quiche provençale 112
- Stuffed artichokes cooked in red wine 82

Omelette
- Pumpkin omelette with cream sauce 108
- Spinach, chickpea and hazelnut omelette 66

Onions
- French onion soup 34
- Pissaladière – Provençal pizza 60
- Ratatouille with roasted potato slices 94

Oranges
- Crêpes with Cointreau cream and oranges 100
- Orange and champagne sorbet 120
- Pear and fennel salad with caramelised nuts and grapes 48
- Vin d'orange 158

P

Parfait
  Raspberry parfait 152
Pears
  Bitter salad with apple and juniper vinaigrette 52
  Carrot, celeriac and pear tarte tatin 110
  Pear and fennel salad with caramelised nuts and grapes 48
  Pear crumble 136
  Stuffed artichokes cooked in red wine 82
Peppers
  Ratatouille with roasted potato slices 94
Pesto
  Caramelised plum tart with Provençal pesto 62
  Provençal pesto 26
Petits fours 130
Pissaladière – Provençal pizza 60
Plums
  Caramelised plum tart with Provençal pesto 62
Potatoes
  Baked asparagus with herb sauce and duchess potatoes 70
  Chestnut soup 38
  Gratin dauphinois 88
  Ratatouille with roasted potato slices 94
  Red cabbage stew 98
  Sauerkraut tart 64
  Stuffed spinach with potato and almond balls 92
Pralines
  Nougat and apricot pralines 126
  Rum truffles 150
Provence-style lentils with cashew cheese 80
Pumpkin
  Lentil and pumpkin stew 74
  Pumpkin omelette with cream sauce 108

Q

Quiche
  Courgette quiche 102
  Quiche provençale 112

R

Raspberries
  Berry and vanilla cream tart 122
  French toast with raspberry sauce 160
  Raspberry liqueur 156
  Raspberry parfait 152
Ratatouille with roasted potato slices 94
Red cabbage
  Red cabbage stew 98
Rum truffles 150

S

Salads
  Bitter salad with apple and juniper vinaigrette 52
  Herbes de Provence and almond terrine with beetroot salad 44
  Pear and fennel salad with caramelised nuts and grapes 48
Sauerkraut
  Sauerkraut tart 64
Sorbet
  Orange and champagne sorbet 120
  Tomato sorbet with basil 54
Soufflé
  Cauliflower soufflé pie 90
Soups
  Chestnut soup 38
  French onion soup 34
  Leek soup 50
  Tomato soup with rosemary foam 36

Spinach
- Baked asparagus with herb sauce and duchess potatoes 70
- Spinach, chickpea and hazelnut omelette 66
- Stuffed spinach with potato and almond balls 92

Strawberries
- Berry and vanilla cream tart 122
- Chocolate and strawberry cream tartlets 132
- Strawberry tart 148

T

Tarts
- Apple and champagne tart 162
- Berry and vanilla cream tart 122
- Caramelised plum tart with Provençal pesto 62
- Carrot, celeriac and pear tarte tatin 110
- Chocolate and strawberry cream tartlets 132
- Grape and yoghurt cream tart 140
- Mushroom and grape tartlets 68
- Sauerkraut tart 64
- Strawberry tart 148
- Tarte tatin 138
- Tomato and cashew cream tart 58

Terrines
- Herbes de Provence and almond terrine with beetroot salad 44
- Vegetable terrine with marinated spring onions 46

Tomatoes
- Aubergine and lemon gratin 86
- Braised fennel with champagne sauce 96
- Lentil and pumpkin stew 74
- Provence-style lentils with cashew cheese 80
- Quiche provençale 112
- Ratatouille with roasted potato slices 94
- Spinach, chickpea and hazelnut omelette 66
- Tomato and cashew cream tart 58
- Tomato sorbet with basil 54
- Tomato soup with rosemary foam 36

Truffles
- Rum truffles 150

V

Vanilla
- Almond biscuits 128
- Apple and champagne tart 162
- Armagnac cake 142
- Berry and vanilla cream tart 122
- Chocolate mousse 118
- Chocolate cake 154
- Coffee crêpe with almonds 104
- Crème Caramel 124
- Crêpes with Cointreau cream and oranges 100
- French toast with raspberry sauce 160
- Grape and yoghurt cream tart 140
- Hazelnut and fig clafoutis 134
- Macarons 146
- Madeleines 144
- Petite fours 130
- Raspberry parfait 152
- Strawberry tart 148
- Vin d'orange 158

Vegetable stock 22

Vinaigrette 26
- Bitter salad with apple and juniper vinaigrette 52
- Porcini mushrooms with walnuts and cranberry vinaigrette 84

W

Walnuts
- Cheese crêpes with walnuts and shallots braised in red wine 106
- Pear and fennel salad with caramelised nuts and grapes 48
- Pear crumble 136
- Porcini mushrooms with walnuts and cranberry vinaigrette 84
- Rum truffles 150

Wine
- Apple and champagne tart 162
- Baguette and vegetable gratin 78
- Caramelised plum tart with Provençal pesto 62
- Cheese crêpes with walnuts and shallots braised in red wine 106
- French onion soup 34
- Red bean and mushroom pie 72
- Red cabbage stew 98
- Stuffed artichokes cooked in red wine 82
- Tomato and cashew cream tart 58
- Vin d'orange 158

Y

Yoghurt
- Grape and yoghurt cream tart 140

THANK YOU

Merci

Many thanks to all the friends who have helped to make this wonderful book and who never tired of sampling the different recipes.

Published in 2022 by
Grub Street
4 Rainham Close
London
SW11 6SS

Email: food@grubstreet.co.uk
Web: www.grubstreet.co.uk
Twitter: @grub_street
Facebook: Grub Street Publishing

Copyright this English language edition © Grub Street 2022

Copyright © Neun Zehn Verlag 2020
Published originally in German as *Vegan Frankreich*
Illustrations: © Henriette Artz
Photography and food styling: © Arnold Pöschl

A CIP catalogue record for this book is available from the British Library.

ISBN 978-1-911667-09-4

The moral right of the author has been asserted.

All rights reserved. Without limiting the rights under copyright reserved above, no part of this publication may be reproduced, stored in or introduced into a retrieval system, or transmitted, in any form or by any means (electronic, mechanical, photocopying, recording or otherwise) without the prior written permission of both the copyright owner and the above publisher of this book.

Printed and bound by Finidr, Czech Republic

OTHER VEGAN TITLES FROM GRUB STREET

VEGAN RECIPES FROM THE MIDDLE EAST
978-1-910690-37-6

VEGAN BBQ
978-1-911621-31-7

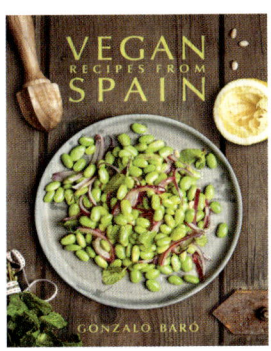

VEGAN RECIPES FROM SPAIN
978-1-911621-16-4

VEGANISSIMO
978-1-911621-40-9

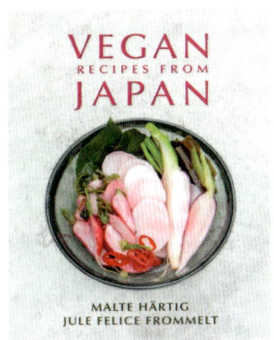

VEGAN RECIPES FROM JAPAN
978-1-911667-04-9

VEGAN BIBLE
978-1-911621-32-4